MW01005434

Answers
to my
Jehovah's
Witness
Friends

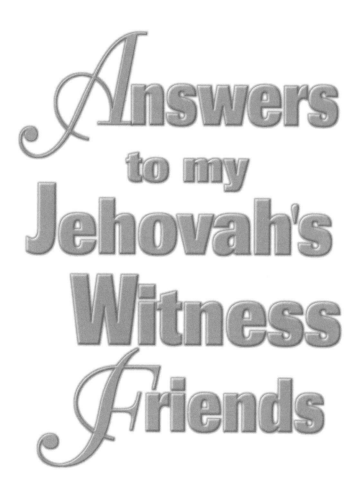

Answers to my Jehovah's Witness Friends

THOMAS F. HEINZE

CHICK
PUBLICATIONS

For a complete list of distributors nearest you call us at (909) 987-0771 or visit us on the world wide web at **www.chick.com**

© 1999 by Thomas F. Heinze
12449 SE Kelly St. • Portland, OR 97236

Cover photo by Tom Myers

Published by:
CHICK PUBLICATIONS
P. O. Box 3500, Ontario, CA 91761-1019 USA
Tel: (909) 987-0771 • Fax: (909) 941-8128
www.chick.com
E Mail: postmaster@chick.com

Printed in the United States of America

ISBN: 0-937958-58-1
Library of Congress Card Catalog Number: 99-75844

Contents

Preface **10**

1 Salvation **13**

   • Follow God's Word Because Men Make Mistakes...................... 14

   • How to Be Born Again 16

   • Works? 18

2 False Prophecy and Mistaken
**   Interpretations of Scripture** **21**

   • 1872 - The Beginning of the Millennium.................................... 24

   • 1975 - Millennium to Begin 25

   • 1874 - Christ's Second Coming According to Pastor Russell 26

   • Christ's Second Coming According to the Bible 27

   • What Does the Bible Tell Us to Do when
     Someone Says Christ Has Come in a
     Secret Way That People Can't See? 28

   • 1914 and 1915 - "The End of the War Which Would
     Destroy the Kingdoms of this World, and Fully
     Establish the Kingdom of God" 28

   • The 1914 Prophecies Were Declared Wrong 31

   • Summary of Dates Set While Watchtower
     Teachings Were Being Established 32

   • So What? 32

   • 1918 - End of Gentile Times, Churches Destroyed 34

   • The 1918 Prophecies Were Declared Wrong 34

   • 1920 - Mountains, Republics, and Kingdoms Disappear 34

   • 1925 - Kingdom Established in Palestine,
     Faithful Men of the Old Testament Return 35

   • The 1925 Prophecies Were Wrong (Also 1914 and 1918) 35

- 1929 - A House Was Built for the Return
  of the Old Testament Faithful 36
- 1932 - The Overthrow of Christendom 37
- 1975 - Beginning of the Millennium 37
- Conclusion: False Prophecies Show
  Inability to Interpret Scripture 37
- Brief Summary of Watchtower dates 39
- What Comes Next? 40

3 The Saved Go To Heaven **41**

- Passages on Heaven 42
- Three of the Beatitudes in Matthew
  Chapter Five Promise Heaven 44
- Believers in Christ Go To Be With
  Him and His Father 44
- Where are Christ and His Father? 45
- Which Should We Desire, Heaven or Earth? 46
- While Our Eternal Home Is Not this Earth, We Have
  Two Types of Promises Regarding the Earth............................. 46
- The Objection, the 144,000 47
  - *Who Are the 144,000?* 48
  - *The 144,000 Are Not the Only Ones in Heaven* 49
  - *A Great Multitude in Heaven* 50
- God is Not Dividing the Saved into Two Groups 52

4 Eternal Punishment **53**

- People Will Share the Eternal
  Punishment of the Devil 54
- Many Other Passages in the New Testament
  Speak of Eternal Punishment 55
- Eternal Punishment in the Old Testament 57
- Hades, and How to Avoid Going There 57

5 How to Interpret the Bible **61**

- Context 62
- Interpret the Unclear in the Light of the Clear 63
- Figurative Language 64

6 Jesus Christ 65

- Is Jesus Christ God? 66
- Christ is called God in the New Testament 67
- "And the Word was God" 67
- Does "a god" Equal "Jehovah?" 68
- Why Does the Bible call Christ Both God and Man? 69
- Christ and the Father Are One 69
- The Words "God" and "Christ" Are
  Used Interchangeably 70
- "Lord of lords and King of kings" 70
- Christ's Works 71
- The Old Testament Foretold Christ's Divinity 72
- Both Christ and His Father Were Called "I Am" 73
- Jesus Christ is Jehovah 73
- Only One Can Be the First and the Last. That
  One Is Called Both Jesus and Jehovah! 74
- Two Pairs of Passages in Revelation 74
  - *The First Pair Is in Chapter One* 75
  - *The Second Pair Is in Chapters 21-22* 76
- John the Baptist Prepared the Way of Jehovah 77
- There Is Only One Savior: Jehovah.
  This One Savior Is also Called Jesus 79
- Arguments to the Contrary 80
- Whose Witnesses Should We Be? 80

7 The Resurrection of Jesus 82

- Jesus Christ Stated That He Would Raise His Body 82
- After the Resurrection, Jesus Claimed that
  His Body Had Been Raised and Proved it.............................. 84
- What Should Our Witness Be? 86
- What Was the Witness of the Apostles? 86
- Your Salvation Depends on Christ's Resurrection 87
- Arguments to the Contrary 89
- How Did Christ Raise Others? 90
- How Can Your Body Be Raised? 90
- Jehovah's Witness Leaders Believe in Bodily Resurrection 91

8 The Holy Spirit 93

• The Holy Spirit Is a Person, Not Just a Force 94

    • *He Does All the Things That Distinguish*
      a Person from a Force 94

    • *Forces Don't Know and Teach,*
      The Spirit Does 94

    • *The Spirit Has Emotions, Forces Don't* 94

    • *The Spirit Speaks* 95

    • *The Spirit Gave the Ability to* 95
      Speak in Foreign Languages

    • *The Spirit Guides* 95

    • *The Spirit Ordains* 96

    • *What Else Might a Person Do?* 96

    • *Arguments to the Contrary* 96

• The Holy Spirit is God 97

    • *His Divinity is Stated* 97

    • *His Divinity Is Demonstrated* 97

    • *The Spirit of God Is the Spirit of Christ, and*
      Only Those in Whom He Dwells Are Saved 98

9 The Trinity 99

• When the Bible Puts the Father, Son, and
  Holy Spirit on the Same Level in the Same
  Scripture, It Shows Us the Trinity 99

• Christ and the Father Are Not Separate
  Gods, They Have the Same Spirit 100

• The Attributes (or Characteristics) of God Belong
  to the Father, the Son, and the Holy Spirit 101

• The Works of God Are Likewise Attributed
  to All Three Persons 101

• God Speaks in the Plural 101

• Each of the Three Persons Is God 102

10 The Name "Jehovah" 103

• The Significance of "Jehovah" 103

• "I Am" and "Jehovah" Used Interchangeably 103

• Jesus Identified Himself with Jehovah 104

- Old Testament Prophecies Equated
  Jehovah with Christ 105
- It Is Not Wrong to Call Jehovah by
  His Other Names 105
- "Jehovah" May Be Translated 106
- The Exception, Jehovah in Psalm 34:8
  Is Christ in 1 Peter 2:3. 107
- What Name Is Above Every Other? 108
- Conclusion 108

11 Should We Give Blood? 109

- Blood Was Prohibited Primarily to the Jews 110
- Gentiles Who Lived with the Jews Were
  Also Prohibited from Eating Blood 110
- Other Gentiles Could Eat Blood 111
- Which Are You? 111
- The Reason for the Law about Blood 111
- May We Eat Blood Now? 113
- The Decision of the Apostles 114
- Before the Law 114
- Transfusions 115
- Love Fulfills the Whole Law 118
- Be a Good Neighbor 119

12 Your Key to the Kingdom 121

- Good Works Don't Save. The Savior Saves! 122
- A Second Chance? 123
- The Reason We Cannot Earn Any of Our
  Salvation Is That It Is a Gift of God 124
- We Receive God's Gift of Salvation
  through Faith in Jesus Christ 124
- A Purified Life Is the Result, Not
  the Cause of Salvation 125
- Act! 125

Preface

All scripture is given by inspiration of God, and is profitable for doctrine, for reproof, for correction, for instruction in righteousness: That the man of God may be perfect, thoroughly furnished unto all good works. 2 Tim. 3:16-17

Jehovah's Witnesses often work with Bible believing Protestant Christians and need to know what we believe. Just as I was not content to learn the teachings of the Jehovah's Witnesses from people who did not believe them, Witnesses need to see for themselves what we believe. Personally studying these beliefs has been encouraged in Watchtower publications:

> "We need to examine, not only what we personally believe, but also what is taught by any religious organization with which we may be associated. Are its teachings in full harmony with God's Word, or are they based on the traditions of men? If we are lovers of the truth, there is nothing to fear from such an examination."[1]

To help you understand what Bible believing Protestants teach, I have gathered together passages from all over the Bible that have determined our beliefs, particularly in the

[1]C.T. Russell, *Studies in the Scriptures,* Vol. 2, "The Time Is At Hand," 1913 Edition, p. 242.

points where they differ with those of the Jehovah's Witnesses. Apply the Watchtower criterion just quoted and judge for yourself whether our position is "in full harmony with God's Word," or "based on the traditions of men," but, whatever conclusion you may come to, you will find studying our beliefs to be interesting and helpful Bible study.

Remember the Watchtower reassurance, "If we are lovers of the truth, there is nothing to fear from such an examination."

One of my goals has been to organize the various subjects in this book in a way that will be handy for you to use. Each chapter is a different subject, so after you have read the book, it will be easy for you to find any topic you wish whenever you need it. I have tried to present each subject in a "friend helping a friend" kind of a way.

In addition to being a direct help to Jehovah's Witnesses who often work with people of our beliefs and need to understand us, I also want to help others of my own persuasion to be better able to give a courteous friendly answer to the Jehovah's Witnesses they meet.

The Scripture passages quoted in this book are from the same Bible used by the Watchtower Society in its early days – the Authorized Version (also known as the King James Version), a translation which is respected by all of us. If you prefer another version, by all means, look the passages up there. I also refer on occasion to the Watch Tower's version, the New World Translation. If you know the original Old Testament Hebrew and New Testament Greek, by all means read the passages there as I have done.

The apostle Paul held up the church in Berea as an

example for us to follow because its people "searched the scriptures daily," to see if the things Paul himself had taught them were the truth (Acts 17:11). Check what I have written that way too. Let's not put any man's word above God's word. That would make a strong statement to Jehovah about what we think of Him!

I have often emphasized in bold the part of a passage most important to the subject being considered so you can see at a glance why I have used the verse. In addition, to keep the book a manageable size, I have only included the phrases from the Bible which are most pertinent to each subject, indicating with three dots (…) any places where phrases less specific to the theme under examination were left out. Don't take my word as to what the passages mean. Read the verses in your own Bible, along with those that come before and after those that I have cited to see that I am not taking things out of context or twisting the meaning.

Now let's examine God's answer to man's most important question.

Except a man be born again, he cannot see the kingdom of God. John 3:3

1

Salvation

After the resurrection, today's Jehovah's Witnesses expect to live in a new paradise on earth under God's reign, because they feel that only 144,000 of the saved will go to heaven.

The Bible teaches that some will be saved and others not. When you talk to people about spiritual things, if someone were to ask you how he could be one of those who will be saved, could you answer him from the Bible?

God's Word says that the Scripture alone has all that it takes to bring us to perfection:

"All scripture is given by inspiration of God, and is profitable for doctrine, for reproof, for correction, for instruction in righteousness, that the man of God may be perfect, thoroughly furnished unto all good works" (2 Tim. 3:16-17).

It follows, therefore, that we should be able to answer the question of how one can be saved from the Bible alone without resorting to men's teachings. If we can't, how do we know that we ourselves will even be counted among God's people?

While Jehovah's Witnesses do not expect to enter God's heavenly reign after death, they want very much to be where He rules on earth. God explains that there is something that must happen before a person can even see a place where He rules: **"Except a man be born again, he cannot see the kingdom of God"** (John 3:3).

The Jehovah's Witnesses have complicated the issue by teaching that the Bible says that only 144,000 people will be born again and go to heaven. This is Jehovah's Witness doctrine, but no passage in the Bible presents or infers this teaching (See chapter 3). Following the teachings of their leaders, however, many Witnesses believe that after the resurrection they will be God's subjects in a new paradise on earth, and that they can enter without being born again. God says the opposite, **"Except a man be born again, he cannot see the kingdom of God"** (John 3:3).

Two verses ahead, John 3:5 repeats the thought in another way, **"… he cannot enter into the kingdom of God."** God's word allows no other means of entrance into any place where He reigns. The next verse explains that the rebirth is spiritual, rather than physical. "What has been born from the flesh is flesh and what has been born from the spirit is spirit" (John 3:6).

Follow God's Word Because
Men Make Mistakes

Pastor Russell, the founder of the Jehovah's Witnesses, when he revised his book, *The Time is at Hand,* said that he had included a mistaken interpretation in the first edition. He wrote in the author's forward when the book was reprinted:

> "The author acknowledges that in this book he presents the thought that the Lord's saints might expect to be with him in glory at the end of the Gentile Times. This was a natural mistake to fall into... we drew a false conclusion, however, not authorized by the Word of the Lord."[1]

Can we trust Russell's statement that he fell into "a natural mistake?" He and the leaders who followed him did not claim to be infallible. When they realized they had taught doctrinal errors, at times they said so. If we can trust anything they said, we should be able to trust these statements. Therefore, in questions such as how to enter into the paradise where God reigns, when God's Word differs from the teachings of the Jehovah's Witnesses, remember that it is God who will judge. When Christ said, **"Except a man be born again, he cannot see the kingdom of God"** (John 3:3), He said it in a way which leaves no room for exceptions, even though He knew that later some people would claim to be of a lesser class with no need to be born again.

If you asked directions and someone pointed and said, "Go north!" when the right direction was south, no matter how sincere the person was, or how often in the past he had been right, this time he was wrong. Following wrong

[1]C.T. Russell, *Studies in the Scriptures,* Vol. 2, "The Time Is At Hand," 1913 Edition, p. 242.

directions would never get you to your destination. When it comes to our salvation, rejecting the teaching of God to follow the mistakes of men keeps people out of God's kingdom. To get there God says for the third time in five verses, **"…Ye must be born again"** (John 3:7). This third time, the New World Translation, written for Jehovah's Witnesses, makes it even more clear that they are not excluded: "Do not marvel because I told you, **You people** must be born again" (John 3:7). There is no other way for a Jehovah's Witness or any one else to enter, or even see, any place where God reigns, so why not be born again?

How to Be Born Again

Nicodemus wants to understand how to be born again, and asks, "How can these things be?" Jesus explains that our rebirth is accomplished by trusting Him, Jesus Christ, to save us:

> "And as Moses lifted up the serpent in the wilderness, even so must the Son of man be lifted up: That **whosoever believeth in him should not perish, but have eternal life"** (John 3:14-15).

Not just the 144,000, but everyone who believes in Christ to save him will be born again and will receive everlasting life.

In fact, as we have seen in verses three and seven, and will see again in verses 16 to 18, trusting Christ is the only way to be saved. The message of John 3:7, "Ye must be born again," cries out to your heart throughout the passage. It is not just for people of that day. It makes no distinction between an earthly kingdom and a heavenly kingdom and no exception for people who lived after 1914. It says, "whosoever." This is not a matter of trying to win an argument. Your own entrance into paradise or anywhere else where God reigns is at stake as well as the entrance of all those you are trying to help. I urge you to take God's word so seriously that you do not give the benefit of the doubt to people who "draw false conclusions" and make "natural mistakes" but to the word of Jehovah Himself.

Because of its importance in bringing people to salvation, the next verse, John 3:16 has probably been committed to memory by more people than any other Bible passage.

"For God so loved the world, that he gave his only begotten Son, that whosoever believeth in him should not perish, but have everlasting life."

God does not condition our salvation on how many visits we have made, how many books we have distributed, or on our ability to be worthy, but on the Savior's ability to save. Those of us who have trusted in Christ have received everlasting life. We testify to you that we have been born again and our spiritual lives have started. God's solution works! Why not shift your faith from whatever else you have believed, and put it in Jesus Christ. Trust Him to save you. If you do, you too will receive everlasting life. You will be born again and have a place in God's kingdom.

The very next verse explains why Christ came into

the world. Understand it, and many of the Bible's teachings will fall into place and make sense.

"For God sent not his Son into the world to condemn the world; but that the world through him might be saved" (John 3:17).

John 3:18 explains what will happen, not only to those who trust Christ, but also to those who insist on following another way:

"He that believeth on him is not condemned: but he that believeth not is condemned already, because he hath not believed in the name of the only begotten Son of God."

Let God's word convince you to quit trusting in what you have done or hope to do, and trust in Christ. The Bible does not admit a second chance after the resurrection. "...he that believeth not is condemned already." (See also Luke 20:35-36.)

Works?

Those who have been born again, the ones who trust Christ to save them, usually do more good works than other people. Observing this, many have fallen into a natural mistake and jumped to the wrong conclusion. They believed that these people's works must have saved them. This leads them to teach that people can be saved by doing the right works, or that at least the works will contribute something toward their salvation.

This is contrary to the scriptures, and while we will go

into it more fully in the last chapter, let's glance at two of the passages that explain the relationship between faith and works:

> "For by grace are ye saved through faith; and that not of yourselves: **it is the gift of God: Not of works, lest any man should boast"** (Eph. 2:8-9).

I am so convinced of the need to distribute Biblical literature that I directed a Biblical publishing ministry for many years, but neither distributing literature nor other fine works add anything to our salvation, because salvation is a gift that God gives us. We receive this gift through faith in Jesus Christ our Savior. There is no other way we can get it! Jesus said:

> **"I am the way,** the truth, and the life: **no man cometh unto the Father, but by me"** (John 14:6).

Only by trusting Christ to save us can we receive God's gift of salvation and be born again.

And if the blind lead the blind, both shall fall into the ditch. Matthew 15:14

2

False Prophecy and Mistaken Interpretations of Scripture

At this point you may be thinking, "It looks like the Bible teaches that I need to be born again, but I have trusted the Watchtower organization which teaches something entirely different. Could its leaders be wrong?"

Do religious leaders make mistakes in interpreting and teaching the Scriptures? Jehovah's Witnesses have often pointed out unmistakable evidence that many who are not Jehovah's Witnesses do make such mistakes. They have even admitted that they too make mistakes. What then should a person who wants to follow God do? Pastor Russell, founder of the Jehovah's Witnesses, suggested a test to determine which prophets we should not follow:

> "Jehovah, the God of the true prophets, will put all false prophets to shame either by not fulfilling the false prediction of such self-assuming prophets or by having His own prophecies fulfilled in a way opposite to that predicted by the false prophets.

21

False prophets will try to hide their reason for feeling shame by denying who they really are."[1]

Pastor Russell said more than once that God would put the
false prophets to shame by not fulfilling their predictions. Here
are almost the same words from another of his books:

"Jehovah… will put all false prophets to shame
either by not fulfilling the false prediction of such
self-assuming prophets or by having His own
prophecies fulfilled in a way opposite to that predicted by the false prophets."[2]

The founder of the Jehovah's Witnesses said we would be
able to tell who the false prophets were because their prophecies would not come true. Do you believe him?

A later Watchtower book also lays forth several ways of
distinguishing true prophets from false ones:

"The three essentials for establishing the creden-
tials of a true prophet, as given through Moses,
were: The true prophet would speak in Jehovah's
name; the things foretold would come to pass
(Deut. 18:20-22); and his prophesying must promote true worship."[3]

Turning to this passage in Deuteronomy you will
notice that the Scriptural emphasis is on the second of these
essentials, that of the things foretold coming to pass. The pas-

[1]*Paradise Restored To Mankind By Theocracy*, Watchtower Bible
and Tract Society, 1972, pp. 353, 354.
[2]C.T. Russell, *Studies in the Scriptures,* Vol. 2, "The Time Is At Hand,"
Watch Tower Bible and Tract Society, 1889 [not in later editions], p. 239.
[3]*Insight On The Scriptures,* 1988 Vol. 2, p. 696.

sage states that if a prophecy does not come true, the person speaking is a false, and not a true, prophet.

Since Pastor Russell and the other Watchtower Society leaders made many prophecies of things that were to happen on specific dates which have now passed, we should do as they said and see if God fulfilled their prophecies. You have nothing to fear if you obey these Watchtower leaders in this Biblical test that they propose. If they check out as true prophets, any doubts you may have had will be laid to rest. If they don't, the sooner you find out the better. If they don't, remember also the last part of the test in our first quote from Pastor Russell. "False prophets will try to hide their reason for feeling shame by denying who they really are." Watch for present day denials that these were intended as prophecies. Watch for attempts to switch something that did happen for the event that was prophesied so people won't notice the failure.

The majority of the teachings the Jehovah's Witnesses still follow today were developed by men who were making predictions complete with dates. These prophecies were made at the same time they were developing Jehovah's Witness doctrine. Since these dates have already passed, they provide an unusual opportunity to find out how accurate these men were in interpreting the Scriptures. Were they always right? Were they ever right? You can use their tests to decide for yourself!

The Bible commends the church in Berea because the people of that church, "received the word with all readiness of mind, and searched the Scriptures daily, whether these things were so" (Acts 17:11). This test is slightly different than the others we have considered. Here the Bible approves the actions of people who were, "examining the Scriptures daily," to see if what the apostle Paul himself taught them agreed with the Bible (See also Psalm 1, 1 John 4:1).

Satan will not want you to make this Biblical test because, "He is a liar and the father of the lie." He may try to make you feel uncomfortable about examining the Scriptures to see for yourself if what you have been taught is true, but listen to God and not to him.

Following this paragraph are quotes from books by Pastor Russell, Judge Rutherford and others who established the teachings of the Jehovah's Witnesses. Most of the predictions of these men were based on their interpretations of the Scriptures. They give actual dates and tell what was to happen when the dates came. The dates are now passed, and these prophecies were either true or false. You can see whether or not their interpretations of the Scriptures can be trusted.

1872 – The Beginning of the Millennium

Pastor Russell declared the millennium to have come in 1872, but when time had passed, it became obvious that the millennium had not come in 1872, and later Watchtower publications predicted that it would come in 1975. Was one of these dates right?

> "In this chapter we present the Bible evidence which indicates that six thousand years from the creation of Adam were complete with A.D. 1872; and hence that, since 1872 A. D., we are chronologically entered upon the seventh thousand or the Millennium—the forepart of which, the "Day of the Lord," the "day of trouble," is to witness the

breaking into pieces of the kingdoms of this world and the establishment of the Kingdom of God under the whole heavens."[1]

It eventually became obvious that the millennium had not really come in 1872, so this date was changed to 1975.

1975 – Millennium to Begin

"According to this trustworthy Bible chronology six thousand years from man's creation will end in 1975, and the seventh period of a thousand years of human history will begin in the fall of 1975 C.E."[2]

Who was right, Pastor Russell who said the millennium had come in 1872, or the later leaders who predicted 1975? The seventh thousand years could not start in 1975 if they had already started in 1872, over 100 years earlier.

1975 passed and with it the hope of many Jehovah's Witnesses who had believed the prophecy. What do you think? Is the battle of Armageddon over? Has Satan been bound? Are you in the millennium now, or were they wrong both times?

[1]C.T. Russell, *Studies in the Scriptures,* Vol. 2, "The Time Is At Hand," Watch Tower Bible and Tract Society, 1909 and 1913 Editions, p. 33, 242. See also *Thy Kingdom Come,* Watch Tower Bible and Tract Society, 1905, p. 127.
[2]*Life Everlasting in Freedom of the Sons of God,* Watch Tower Bible and Tract Society, 1966, p. 29. (Date also listed in chart on page 35.) See also *The Watchtower,* 10/15/69, p. 623; *The Approaching Peace of a Thousand Years,* p. 26-27; *Kingdom Ministry,* March, 1968 p. 4).

Now that we have compared the statements about 1872 and 1975, we will examine the rest of the dates in chronological order starting with 1874.

1874 – Christ's Second Coming According to Pastor Russell

Pastor Russell stated: "The second coming of the Lord, therefore began in 1874." This was two years after the date he had given for the beginning of the millennium.

> "The second coming of the Lord therefore began in 1874; and that date and the years 1914 to 1918 are specially marked dates with reference to his coming."[1]

This was considered important and was repeated in several ways in a number of books.

> "The Scriptural proof is that the second presence of the Lord Jesus Christ began in 1874 A.D."[2]

There were no tangible evidences of Christ having come in 1874, but Pastor Russell believed it anyway:

> "Surely there is not the slightest room for doubt in

[1] J. F. Rutherford, *Creation,* Watch Tower Bible and Tract Society, 1927, p. 310.

[2] J. F. Rutherford, *Prophecy,* Watch Tower Bible and Tract Society, 1929 p. 65. See also: *Thy Kingdom Come,* Watch Tower Bible and Tract Society, 1891, 1923, p. 235; *The Battle of Armageddon,* Watch Tower Bible and Tract Society, 1897, 1913, p. 621; C.T. Russell, *Studies in the Scriptures,* Vol. 7, "The Finished Mystery," Watch Tower Bible and Tract Society, p. 58.

the mind of a truly consecrated child of God that the Lord Jesus is present and has been since 1874."[1]

Christ's Second Coming According to the Bible

Since God's word clearly describes Christ's second coming, we can compare what it says with the happenings of the year 1874 and following to find out whether the Lord actually came then or not. Here is the Bible's description of the second coming of Jesus Christ:

• "Behold, he cometh with clouds; and **every eye shall see him"** (Rev. 1:7).

• "…Ye men of Galilee, why stand ye gazing up into heaven? this same Jesus, which is taken up from you into heaven, shall so come in like manner as ye have seen him go into heaven" (Acts 1:11).

• "And then shall appear the sign of the Son of man in heaven: and then shall all the tribes of the earth mourn, and **they shall see the Son of man coming in the clouds of heaven with power and great glory"** (Matt. 24:30). See also Mark 13:26; Luke 21:27; 2 Thess. 1:6-10.

Did any of these things actually happen in 1872, 1874, 1914, 1918, or even in 1975? The Scriptures are clear. There will be no doubt when Christ comes again! His coming will be visible to all and will attract attention.

[1]Watchtower, Jan. 1, 1924, p. 5.

What Does the Bible Tell Us to Do When Someone Says Christ Has Come in a Secret Way That People Can't See?

"Then if any man shall say unto you, Lo, here is Christ, or there; believe it not. For there shall arise false Christs, and false prophets, and shall shew great signs and wonders; insomuch that, if it were possible, they shall deceive the very elect. Behold, I have told you before. Wherefore if they shall say unto you, Behold, he is in the desert; go not forth: behold, he is in the secret chambers; believe it not. For as the lightning cometh out of the east, and shineth even unto the west; so shall also the coming of the Son of man be" (Matt. 24:23-27, 30). See also Luke 17:23-24.

Pastor Russell's explanation of an invisible coming that leaves no evidence is just what the Bible says not to believe. He has put us in a difficult position. We find ourselves commanded by God not to believe him!

1914 and 1915 – "The End of the War Which Would Destroy the Kingdoms of this World, and Fully Establish the Kingdom of God"

(When this did not happen in 1914, the date was changed to 1915.)

As you read the quotes of these prophecies, note that these were prophecies of the *end* of a war which would replace the governments of men with the government of God, and not predictions of the First World War which *began* in 1914, and

ended in 1918 without having replaced the world's governments with God's government. What actually did happen in
1914, in spite of its importance, seems to have been entirely
unforeseen by the Watchtower prophets. Since something
important did happen in 1914, people today sometimes try to
infer that the prophecy was fulfilled. At the time, however, the
Watchtower leadership did not promote that interpretation.

On the contrary, they changed the date to 1915, showing
that they understood that the things prophesied for 1914 had
not happened. The Watchtower publications made clear the
fact that the 1914 prophecies were wrong. Notice both that
what was to happen did not, and that the date changes from
1914 to 1915 in different editions of the same book.

1909 edition:

"True, it is expecting great things to claim, as
we do, that within the coming twenty-six years all
present governments will be overthrown and dissolved;"

"...In view of this strong Bible evidence concerning the Times of the Gentiles, we consider it an
established truth that the final end of the kingdoms
of this world, and the full establishment of the
Kingdom of God, will be accomplished at the end
of A.D. 1914. Then the prayer of the Church,
ever since her Lord took his departure— 'Thy
Kingdom, come'–will be answered; and under that
wise and just administration, the whole earth will
be filled with the glory of the Lord—with knowledge, and righteousness, and peace (Psa. 72:19;

Isa. 6:3; Hab. 2:14); and the will of God shall be done *'on earth, as it is done in heaven.'*"[1]

1914 passed and the Watchtower association had to deal with the fact that it had brought neither "the final end of the kingdoms of this world," nor "the full establishment of the kingdom of God." In the 1915 edition, therefore, the date was changed from 1914 to 1915, but with no better luck. I quote here from the 1919 reprint of the 1915 edition which admits in the introduction, "…we drew a false conclusion, however, not authorized by the Word of the Lord."

1915 edition:

"True, it is expecting great things to claim, as we do, that within the coming twenty-six years all present governments will be overthrown and dissolved;"

"…In view of this strong Bible evidence concerning the Times of the Gentiles, we consider it an established truth that the final end of the kingdoms of this world, and the full establishment of the Kingdom of God, will be accomplished at the end of A.D. 1915. Then the prayer of the Church, ever since her Lord took his departure— 'Thy Kingdom, come'—will be and under that wise and just administration, the whole earth will be filled with the glory of the Lord—with knowledge, and

---

[1]C.T. Russell, *Studies in the Scriptures,* Vol. 2, "The Time is at Hand", 1889 and 1909 edition, Watch Tower Bible and Tract Society, p. 99. See also: ppg. 76-77, 101, 245.

righteousness, and peace (Psa. 72:19; Isa. 6:3; Hab. 2:14); and the will of God shall be done 'on earth, as it is done in heaven.'"[1]

The 1914 Prophecies Were Declared Wrong:

"The Watch Tower, and its companion publications of the Society, for forty years emphasized the fact that 1914 would witness the establishment of God's kingdom and the complete glorification of the church. During that period of forty years God's people on earth were carrying on a witness work, which work was foreshadowed by Elijah and John the Baptist. All of the Lord's people looked forward to 1914 with joyful expectation. When that time came and passed there was much disappointment, chagrin and mourning, and the Lord's people were greatly in reproach. They were ridiculed by the clergy and their allies in particular, and pointed to with scorn, because they had said so much about 1914, and what would come to pass, and their 'prophecies' had not been fulfilled."[2]

Sometimes when their prophesies proved to be false, as in the quote above, later Watchtower publications admitted it. Other times, as in the quote which follows, they tried to escape the blame, inferring that the followers rather than the leaders had made the mistake.

---

[1]Ibid., 1919 reprint of the 1915 edition, p. 99.
[2]J. F. Rutherford, *Light, Book 1,* Watch Tower Bible and Tract Society, 1930, p. 194. See also ppg. 136,194-195.

"Many of such had been looking for the Lord to come and take them to heaven, and had particularly fixed the year 1914 as when this should be done. The year 1914 *was* a marked date; but these had merely contemplated something to happen which did not come to pass."[1]

Summary of Dates Set While Watchtower Teachings Were Being Established

• **1872** Beginning of the millennium. Wrong! Because the millennium did not start in 1872, later Watchtower publications changed the date to 1975, another date in which it did not happen.

• **1874** Christ's second coming. Nothing happened. The Bible says His second coming will be visible to all.

• **1914** All world governments to be overthrown. God will start to govern the world and His people will be glorified. When it did not happen, the date was changed to 1915.

• **1915** The Watchtower society later admitted that its prophesies about 1914 and 1915 "had not been fulfilled."

So What?

The people who made these false prophecies claimed that they had based most of them on Scripture. Their obvious errors in these prophecies included dates

---

[1]J. F. Rutherford, *Prophecy,* Watch Tower Bible and Tract Society, 1929, p. 89.

which can easily be checked. When we check these dates, it is clear that the prophecies did not come to pass because they did not interpret the Scriptures correctly.

Look out! The interpretations of these same people are the basis for almost all of the doctrines of the Jehovah's Witnesses. Since they were wrong where they could be put to the test, why should you believe what they teach in areas that you can't check as easily?

I once helped a blind man get an operation that gave him sight. When we heard of a doctor who performed a new operation that might help his kind of blindness, his first move was to go to a meeting of blind people and ask them about this doctor's record as a surgeon. Everyone he found that this man had operated on was still blind! He then asked if there were other doctors who also performed this new operation and found that there was one who was an expert. This surgeon had been successful in every case in which he could be checked. My friend came back to me with this information. If you were I, which doctor would you have taken him to?

Will you follow doctors of religion who were wrong wherever you could put them to the test?

Did the ability of the Watchtower prophets to predict dates improve from here on? No, but our purpose in this investigation was to see if the people who established the Watchtower doctrines were reliable in their interpretation of Scripture. After 1915, most of the Watchtower doctrines had already been established, so to save space we will treat the rest of the prophetic dates more briefly.

More Recent Dates
1918 – End of Gentile Times, Churches Destroyed

Churches and church members were to be destroyed in 1918 and Jehovah's Witnesses glorified.[1]

The 1918 Prophecies Were Declared Wrong:

"However, suddenly, there came an end to World War I. It did not lead on, as Bible students expected, into world revolution and anarchy or the battle of Armageddon. And the sincere worshippers of Jehovah, who were in the new covenant with him through his Mediator Jesus Christ, found themselves still in the flesh on the earth."[2]

1920 – Mountains, Republics, and Kingdoms Disappear

"And the mountains were not found. Even the republics will disappear in the fall of 1920. And the mountains were not found. Every kingdom of earth will pass away, be swallowed up in anarchy."[3]

[1]*The Finished Mystery,* Watch Tower Bible and Tract Society, 1917 edition, p. 404,485.

[2]*Man's Salvation Out Of World Distress At Hand*, Watch Tower Bible and Tract Society, 1975; p. 98. See also p. 136.

[3]C.T. Russell, *Studies In The Scriptures,* Vol. 7, "The Finished Mystery," Watch Tower Bible and Tract Society, 1917 edition, p. 258.

1925 – Kingdom Established in Palestine, Faithful Men of the Old Testament Return

"Therefore we may confidently expect that 1925 will mark the return of Abraham, Isaac, Jacob and the faithful prophets of old…"[1]

"…there is evidence that the establishment of the Kingdom in Palestine will probably be in 1925, ten years later than we once calculated."[2]

"There will be no slip-up… Abraham should enter upon the actual possession of his promised inheritance in the year 1925."[3]

The 1925 Prophecies Were Wrong
(Also 1914 and 1918)

"God's faithful people on the earth emphasized the importance of the dates 1914 and 1918 and 1925. They had much to say about these dates and what would come to pass, but all they predicted did not come to pass."[4]

---

[1]*Millions Now Living Will Never Die,* 1918, p. 89. See also ppg. 90, 97. Golden Age, Jan. 4, 1922, p. 217.

[2]C.T. Russell, *Studies In The Scriptures,* Vol. 7, "The Finished Mystery," Watch Tower Bible and Tract Society, 1917 edition, p. 128.

[3]Watchtower, Oct. 15, 1917, p. 6157.

[4]J. F. Rutherford, *Vindication,* book one, Watch Tower Bible and Tract Society, 1931, p. 146. See also Yearbook, 1975, p. 146. *Watchtower,* Nov. 1, 1993, p. 12.

1929 – A House Was Built for the Return of the Old Testament Faithful

"At San Diego, California, there is a small piece of land, on which, in the year 1929, there was built a house, which is called and known as Beth-Sarim. The Hebrew words *Beth Sarim*

mean "House of the Princes"; and the purpose of acquiring that property and building the house was that there might be some tangible proof that there are those on earth today who fully believe God and Christ Jesus and in His kingdom, and who believe that the faithful men of old will soon be resurrected by the Lord, be back on earth, and take charge of the visible affairs of earth. The occupation of the house by the princes was to "be a confirmation of the faith and hope that induced the building of Beth-Sarim."[1]

[1]J. F. Rutherford, *Salvation,* Watch Tower Bible and Tract Society, 1939, ppg. 311-312. See also *The New World,* Watch Tower Bible and Tract Society, 1942, ppg. 104-105.

When it became obvious that the prediction would not be fulfilled, the house became an embarrassing monument to a false prophecy. It was sold in 1948!

1932 – The Overthrow of Christendom

The Prophecy of the Overthrow of Christendom Was Wrong. The Watchtower said:

> "They had preached that in an early time God would overthrow 'Christendom'. Many had emphasized the year 1925 as the date, and then when that date did not materialize the date was moved up to 1932. Again, 1932 came and 'Christendom' was not destroyed…"[1]

1975 – Beginning of the Millennium

Predicting the beginning of the millennium for 1975 made it obvious that the Watchtower leadership no longer considered valid the statement that the millennium had come in 1872. The new date disproved the old. Because of this, I have placed the quotes of the 1975 prophecies right after those for 1872 to make it easier to compare the two. You may turn back to 1872 and read them there (p. 24-25).

Conclusion:

False Prophecies Show Inability to Interpret Scripture. Having seen the false prophecies of the

[1]The Watchtower, Feb. 15, 1938, p. 54.

Watchtower publications for yourself, you realize that the people who formed Jehovah's Witness doctrine have made serious mistakes in their interpretations of Scripture. You know that Pastor Russell, who founded the Jehovah's Witnesses and established many of the doctrines, published prophecies complete with dates. You have seen quotes from his books, and know that the prophecies were wrong. Since they were usually based on his interpretations of Scripture, you know that his interpretations were not reliable. He even admitted making doctrinal mistakes.

Judge Rutherford who followed Pastor Russell in establishing the doctrines of the Jehovah's Witnesses, also wrote predictions complete with dates based on his interpretations of Scripture. These also check out wrong. Speaking of this after the fact, the Watchtower said,

> "Things published were not perfect in the days of Charles Taze Russell, first president of the Watchtower Bible and Tract Society; nor were they perfect in the days of J. F. Rutherford, the succeeding president. The increasing light on God's Word as well as the facts of history have repeatedly required that adjustments of one kind or another be made down to the very present time."[1]

Therefore, when one of these men's followers suggests that you should not read the Bible by itself, apart from their interpretations, or that you should not read explanations other than those of the Watchtower Society, don't give in to such bad advice. The person who made the suggestion will not take

[1] *The Watchtower,* March 1, 1979, p. 24.

your punishment on himself if your life is ruined by false doctrine. You are responsible for your own decisions and your own actions. The Bible teaches you to check out what others tell you (Acts 17:11). Why would you want to blindly entrust the salvation of your soul to men who were so clearly wrong in the points in which they could be easily checked? You have God's word in your hand and are responsible to see for yourself what He is teaching!

Now that you understand the necessity of independent Bible study, you may want to look up the Scriptures listed in chapter one about how to enter God's kingdom. Find them in your Bible and read them all by themselves, apart from my interpretation or that of anyone else. It is particularly important to understand what the Bible teaches about your salvation.

Brief Summary of Watchtower dates:

• **1872** Beginning of the millennium. Wrong! Watchtower publications later changed the date to 1975, another date in which it did not happen.

• **1874** Christ's second coming. Nothing happened. The Bible says His second coming will be seen by all.

• **1914** All world governments to be overthrown. God will glorify His people and govern the world.

• **1915** When man's governments were not replaced by God's in 1914, the date was changed to 1915. The Watchtower Society later admitted these prophecies "had not been fulfilled."

- **1918** End of Gentile times, the churches to be destroyed.
- **1920** The mountains, republics, and kingdoms were to disappear.
- **1925** The kingdom was to be established in Palestine. Faithful men of the Old Testament were to return. It was later admitted that this and the 1918 prediction were wrong.
- **1929** A house was built for the return of the Old Testament faithful. It was sold in 1948 because they did not return.
- **1932** The Watchtower stated that the date for the overthrow of Christendom had been moved up from 1925 (previously 1918) to 1932 and that the overthrow did not happen in 1932 either.
- **1975** Since the Millennium had not begun in 1872, the date was changed to 1975. Again nothing happened.

What Comes Next?

Chapter three will let you see from the Bible alone where the saved go after death. If you have been following the views of men who say there is no way you can get into heaven, you will find the Bible's teaching a very pleasant surprise.

Rejoice, and be exceeding glad: for great is your reward in heaven. Matthew 5:12

3

The Saved Go To Heaven

Jehovah's Witnesses teach that when they die they will be resurrected to life on earth, and that only the 144,000 will go to heaven. The Bible's teaching on where the saved go after death is so different from that of the men who formed the Jehovah's Witnesses' doctrines that you may find this chapter hard to accept. I first realized just how hard when one of my sons came to me and said, "Dad, a Jehovah's Witness gets on the train at a stop after mine and always sits by me and talks about their teachings till I get off to go to my school. Today, he said, 'Those who are saved in our times don't go to heaven, but to an earthly kingdom.' Could you find me some verses that say that the saved go to heaven?"

I did, and wrote them out for him with a bit of explanation. He gave them to his friend the next day on the train. From that day on, this person never sat by him again or even looked his way. This has helped me realize how sensitive a point this can be. Since I don't want to offend you who are reading, I will just copy most of the verses on heaven without explaining them at all, in order that you may determine for yourself what God is teaching. By not inserting my comments, I hope that you will not be offended but will, "Rejoice, and be exceeding glad: for great is your reward in heaven" (Matt. 5:12).

There are quite a number of passages, so for brevity, I will just give the parts which deal directly with the subject at hand, emphasizing in bold the most important phrases, but suggest that you read these Scriptures in your own Bible together with the verses that surround them which often help determine their meaning.

Jehovah's Witnesses have usually been convinced that only the 144,000 will go to heaven. This is the opposite of what the Bible teaches. I go over all of the passages that mention the 144,000 at the end of this chapter. If you need to, you can read that part first, but do come back.

Passages on Heaven

"And I say unto you, that many shall come from the east and west, and shall sit down with Abraham, and Isaac, and Jacob, **in the kingdom of heaven.**"

(Matt. 8:11)

"Blessed be the God and Father of our Lord Jesus Christ, which according to his abundant mercy hath begotten us again unto a lively hope by the resurrection of Jesus Christ from the dead, to an inheritance incorruptible, and undefiled, and that fadeth not away, **reserved in heaven for you**" (1 Pet. 1:3-4).

"…for the things which are seen are temporal; but the things which are not seen are eternal. For we know that if our earthly house of this tabernacle were dissolved, **we have a building of God, a house not made with hands, eternal in the heavens.** For in this we groan, earnestly desiring to be clothed upon with our house which is from heaven" (2 Cor. 4:18-5:2).

"For our conversation is in heaven…" (Phil. 3:20).

But notice how the New World Translation renders this: "As for us, our citizenship exists in the heavens…")

"For the hope which is laid up for you in heaven…"
(Col. 1:5)

"Rejoice ye in that day, and leap for joy: for, behold, **your reward is great in heaven"** (Luke 6:23).

"But now they desire a better country, that is, an heavenly…" (Heb. 11:16).

"For when they shall rise from the dead, they neither marry, nor are given in marriage; but are as the angels which are in heaven" (Mark 12:25).

The words "which are" are not in the Greek, but even if they were, why would those who are raised from the dead be equipped for heaven if their destiny is earth?

"And the Lord shall deliver me from every evil work, and will preserve me **unto his heavenly kingdom"** (2 Tim. 4:18).

The word translated "unto" is the normal Greek word for "into." See the word so translated twice in Matthew 9:17.

"Except ye be converted, and become as little children, ye shall not enter into the kingdom of heaven" (Matt. 18:3).

Three of the Beatitudes in Matthew Chapter Five Promise Heaven

• "Blessed are the poor in spirit: for **theirs is the kingdom of heaven"** (Matt. 5:3).

• "Blessed are they which are persecuted for righteousness' sake: for **theirs is the kingdom of heaven"** (Matt. 5:10).

• "Rejoice, and be exceeding glad: for great is your reward in heaven" (Matt. 5:12).

Believers in Christ Go To Be With Him and His Father

Jesus prepared a place for the believers where they would be with Him and His Father:

"In my Father's house are many mansions: if it were not so, I would have told you. I go to prepare a place for you. And if I go and prepare a place for you, I will come again, and receive you unto myself; **that where I am, there ye may be also.** And whither I go ye know, and the way ye know. Thomas saith unto him, Lord, we know not whither thou goest; and how can we know the way? Jesus saith unto him, I am the way, the truth, and the life: no man cometh unto the Father, but by me" (John 14:2-6).

Where are Christ and His Father?

Where is this place with many abodes which Christ prepared for us where His father is?

"Our Father which art **in heaven**" (Matt. 6:9).

See also Matt. 5:16, 48; 6:1; 7:11.

In another prayer, Jesus asked that his followers would be where he was and he with the Father.

"And now, O Father, glorify thou me with thine own self with the glory which I had with thee before the world was" (John 17:5).

"I will that they also, whom thou hast given me, be with me where I am" (John 17:24).

"For Christ is not entered into the holy places made with hands, which are the figures of the true; but **into heaven itself, now to appear in the presence of God** for us" (Heb. 9:24).

"And it came to pass, while he blessed them, he was parted from them, and **carried up into heaven."**

(Luke 24:51)

"…by the resurrection of Jesus Christ: Who is gone into heaven, and is on the right hand of God."

(1 Pet. 3:21-22)

One day Jesus will return from heaven:

"For the Lord himself shall **descend from heaven** with a shout, with the voice of the archangel, and with the trump of God: and the dead in Christ shall rise first. Then we which are alive and remain shall be **caught up together with them in the clouds, to meet the Lord in the air: and so shall we ever be with the Lord"** (1 Thess. 4:16-17).

Which Should We Desire, Heaven or Earth?

If you are a Jehovah's Witness, you have probably been taught not to desire to go to heaven, but to a paradise on earth. The Bible teaches:

"Lay not up for yourselves treasures upon earth, where moth and rust doth corrupt, and where thieves break through and steal, but **lay up for yourselves treasures in heaven,** where neither moth nor rust doth corrupt, and where thieves do not break through nor steal: for where your treasure is, there will your heart be also" (Matt. 6:19-21).

God wants it to be our hearts to desire to go to heaven with Him, not to be resurrected on earth.

While Our Eternal Home Is Not this Earth, We Have Two Types of Promises Regarding the Earth

• The unrighteous will not prosper for ever in this life on earth because God will step in, eliminate them, and give their land to the just. The just will pass it down as an inheritance to their children after them. Psalm 37 and Matthew 5:5 are examples.

• There will be a period in the future when Christ will reign on the earth for 1000 years (Rev. 20:1-6; Isa. 11:1-10). Don't think that the promise of a period when Christ reigns on earth eliminates the many promises of heaven. The many passages examined above clearly show that a place in heaven has been and is reserved for the saved in general, not for just a few of them. In addition, later, after Christ has ruled as king until God has subjected all things under His feet, He will hand the kingdom over to His Father (1 Cor. 15:24-25).

The Objection, the 144,000

Jehovah's Witnesses often answer that the 144,000 are the only ones who are born again and who will go to heaven, explaining that these are the apostles and the people who became Jehovah's Witnesses before 1914. The Watchtower has taught that some of these early Witnesses would still be alive at the coming of God's kingdom and would pass into it without dying. They consign the rest of the saved to God's earthly kingdom. The Bible, however, clearly states that the 144,000 are Israelites, that is, Jews. They are found only in Revelation 7 and 14. Since only chapter seven deals with who they were, we can easily check this. Let's do it.

Who Are the 144,000?

Chapter 7 clearly states that the 144,000 were sealed from among those on earth for special treatment during the great tribulation, and that they are from each of the twelve tribes of the sons of Israel:

> "And I heard the number of them which were sealed: and there were sealed **an hundred and forty and four thousand of all the tribes of the children of Israel."** (Rev. 7:4)

To reinforce this, the twelve tribes of Israel are then all listed by name, 12,000 from each tribe. It could hardly be stated more clearly that they are Israelites, that is, Jews. Had God been referring to "spiritual" Israel, he could easily have just said so and left out the long list of names of the 12 tribes.

Jehovah's Witnesses believe that the number is not to be taken spiritually, but literally, not "a large number," but exactly 144,000. Of what? Taken literally, the 144,000 were Jews, but Jehovah's Witnesses say that this part should not be taken literally, but spiritually, and means "Spiritual Israel." By this they mean mostly Jehovah's Witnesses with a few apostles and a few other early Christians thrown in. Neither of the two chapters that mention the 144,000 give any foundation at all to this man-made doctrine. While it is true that in this list of the 12 tribes, the descendants of Ephraim, who fell into idolatry, are listed by the name of Ephraim's father Joseph, this in no way infers that any of the 144,000 were Jehovah's Witnesses born before 1914, yet such are the arguments that have been used to back the claim that the 144,000 were not Jews but Jehovah's Witnesses.

The idea that the 144,000, born before 1914, would pass directly into heaven without dying has become ever more difficult to maintain as the years have passed. This quote from the October 8, 1968 issue of *Awake!* makes the problem clear. "Jesus was obviously speaking about those who were old enough to witness with understanding what took place when the 'last days' began… Even if we presume that youngsters 15 years of age would be perceptive enough to realize the import of what happened in 1914, it would still make the youngest of 'this generation' nearly 70 years old today… Jesus said that the end of this wicked world would come before that generation passed away in death."

By 1998, the youngest of "this generation" was 100 years old! It had gradually became obvious that this prophecy would not be fulfilled either, so it too is being abandoned. Let us pray that these facts will give you boldness to put the clear statements of the Bible above the words of fallible men.

The 144,000 Are Not the Only Ones in Heaven

The really important thing about the 144,000 is not that the Watchtower's opinion is changing about whether or not they will pass into heaven without dying, but whether they will be the only ones in heaven. In fact, the two times the Bible mentions them they are on earth. In Revelation 14:1 they are "on the Mount Zion" which is in Jerusalem and hear singing from heaven. In 7:2-3, they are also on earth.

While it might be reasonably inferred that at some later

date they, along with many others would be in heaven, no passage in the Bible says so. Assuming that the Witnesses are not wrong in thinking that the 144,000 will one day be in heaven, a phrase which describes them in 14:4 becomes very important, "These were redeemed from among men, being the **firstfruits** unto God and to the Lamb." The word "firstfruits" in the Bible refers to the first of something that will be followed by many others. Under the law of Moses when the harvest began, the first of the firstfruits were to be offered to the Lord (Ex. 23:19). It taught the people to trust God for the rest of the harvest. If the 144,000 are in heaven as firstfruits, many others will be coming to heaven too.

A Great Multitude in Heaven

In chapter seven, right after explaining that the 144,000 are Jews, the scene changes from the earth where the 144,000 were sealed to heaven. In heaven we are shown a different group of people, an innumerable crowd from all nations and peoples:

> "After this I beheld, and, lo, a great multitude, which no man could number, of all nations, and kindreds, and people, and tongues, stood before the throne, and before the Lamb, clothed with white robes, and palms in their hands. And cried with a loud voice, saying, Salvation to our God which sitteth upon the throne, and unto the Lamb" (Rev. 7:9-10).

The passage states that this great crowd, too big to count, of people from all nations, is standing before the throne of God. Jehovah's Witness' doctrine, in maintaining that the

144,000 are the only ones in heaven, contradicts this clear teaching of the Word of Jehovah!

There is no question that the throne where the great multitude is standing is in heaven, because all of chapter 4 is devoted to God's throne and what goes on around it, "Behold, a throne was set in heaven, and one sat on the throne" (Rev. 4:2). In chapter seven, we find a huge crowd of people of all nationalities (not part of the 144,000 who are Jews) in heaven before the throne.

Please read all of chapters four and seven so your faith will be based on the Scriptures themselves, in context, and not on my having said what a few of the verses teach, or on someone else's mistaken belief that only the 144,000 will be in heaven. Notice that 7:15 repeats that the great multitude clothed in white robes is "before the throne of God, and serve him day and night in his temple". Notice the added information here: "in his temple". This temple is clearly "in heaven" in Revelation 11:19 and 14:17. The 144,000 are certainly not the only ones in heaven, and no passage in the Bible even infers that they might be. The teaching that only they are there is a man made doctrine which contradicts the clear teaching of God's Word that they are firstfruits, and that an innumerable multitude will have washed their robes in the blood of the Lamb and be standing before God's throne in Heaven. An overwhelming number of passages tell us that the believer's hope is in heaven. Remember Christ's command:

> "Lay not up for yourselves treasures upon earth, where moth and rust doth corrupt, and where thieves break

through and steal, but lay up for yourselves treasures in heaven, where neither moth nor rust doth corrupt, and where thieves do not break through nor steal for where your treasure is, there will your heart be also" (Matt. 6:19-21).

God is Not Dividing the Saved into Two Groups

Christ said:

"And other sheep I have, which are not of this fold: them also I must bring, and they shall hear my voice; and **there shall be one fold, and one shepherd"** (John 10:16).

See also John 11:52, Eph. 3:4-6.

God's purpose is just the opposite of maintaining two distinct groups of the saved, one aimed for heaven and the other for earth. It is to bring believers from all nations into one united group. The Biblical evidence is overwhelming. Christ died that those who trust in Him may be with Him and His Father in heaven. Trust the Savior to save you, and and to include you in that group.

The next chapter will help you decide, by considering what will happen if you don't.

"And the smoke of their torment ascendeth up for ever and ever: and they have no rest day nor night." Revelation 14:11

4

Eternal Punishment

Jehovah's Witnesses teach that the unsaved do not go to a place of eternal punishment, but cease to exist. This contradicts any translation of the Bible, including the Watchtower's New World Translation. A place of eternal punishment clearly does exist, and is the destiny of those who refuse the salvation God offers them in Christ, so refusing to accept Christ as Savior is not what you want to do.

Here again, we are faced with the decision of whether to believe the words of men who have made many mistakes, or to believe God's word which says:

"If any man worship the beast and his image, and receive his mark in his forehead, or in his hand, the same shall drink of the wine of the wrath of God, which is poured out without mixture into the cup of his indignation; and **he shall be tormented with fire and brimstone** in the presence of the holy angels, and in the presence of the Lamb: And the smoke of their torment ascendeth up for ever and ever: **and they have no rest day nor night…"**

(Rev. 14:9-11)

There is no way to honestly interpret "and they have no rest day nor night" to mean that these sinners just won't exist any more. The New World Translation puts it: "…and day and night they have no rest."

People Will Share the Eternal Punishment of the Devil

Another passage which clearly shows a place of eternal punishment is talking about the eternal punishment of the devil. It is important to this subject because people will be there sharing his eternal punishment.

"And the devil that deceived them was cast into the lake of fire and brimstone, where the beast and the false prophet are, and shall be **tormented day and night for ever and ever"** (Rev. 20:10).

Here the New World translation translates the phrase which we have put in bold with exactly the same words.

It is Christ Himself who told us that people would share this punishment, "…and he shall separate them one from another." "Then shall he say also unto them on the left hand, 'Depart from me, ye cursed, **into everlasting fire,** prepared for the devil and his angels'" (Matt. 25:31, 41). Read also the context from Matt. 25:31 to 46.

Verse 46 sums up the passage: **"And these shall go**

away into everlasting punishment: but the righteous into life eternal" (Matt. 25:46). In this last verse, in the New World Translation, "punishment" has been substituted by "cutting-off," changing an action which continues forever into an action that is immediately over and done with.

Replacing the normal translation with Watchtower doctrine is not unusual in the New World Translation's treatment of this subject, the divinity of Christ, and to a lesser degree, other points of doctrinal difference. Generally I have chosen to use passages which both the New World and the Authorized Version translated well and have not used the others. Here, however, and in a few other verses, if you use the New World Translation, you will find a significant difference. Please refer to other respected translations or the original Greek or Hebrew if you have any doubts as to which is more accurate in these cases.

Many Other Passages in the New Testament Speak of Eternal Punishment

These verses are similar in New World Translation, in that there too they speak of eternal punishment:

- "The Son of man shall send forth his angels, and they shall gather out of his kingdom all things that offend, and them which do iniquity, and shall cast them into a furnace of fire: **there shall be wailing and gnashing of teeth"** (Matt. 13:41-42).
- "So shall it be at the end of the world: the angels shall come forth, and sever the wicked from among the just,

and shall cast them into the furnace of fire: there shall be **wailing and gnashing of teeth"** (Matt. 13: 49-50).

• "...cast into hell fire where **their worm dieth not, and the fire is not quenched"** (Mark 9:47-48).

It is normal to wish that a place of eternal punishment did not exist. As much as we might prefer this, no matter what translation we read, we can hardly interpret these descriptions as speaking of ceasing to exist rather than continuing punishment, so why go there?

> • "And it came to pass, that the beggar died, and was carried by the angels into Abraham's bosom: the rich man also died, and was buried. And in hell he lift up his eyes, **being in torments,** and seeth Abraham afar off, and Lazarus in his bosom, and he cried and said, Father Abraham, have mercy on me, and send Lazarus, that he may dip the tip of his finger in water, and cool my tongue; for **I am tormented in this flame.** But Abraham said, Son, remember that thou in thy lifetime receivedst thy good things, and likewise Lazarus evil things: but now he is comforted, and **thou art tormented.** And beside all this, between us and you there is a great gulf fixed: so that they which would pass from hence to you cannot; neither can they pass to us, that would come from thence" (Luke 16:22-26).

Jehovah's Witnesses often say that this passage is not to be taken literally, but is a parable. If this is true, it should strike terror in the hearts of those who are not born again, because Christ's parables were stories that taught truths and this story obviously teaches that the lost are conscious after death and suffer. Read also the following verses, which teach that people who don't believe the Scriptures, will not repent even if someone should rise from the dead to warn them, a reference to the obstinate people who did not believe and repent even though Christ Himself rose from the dead and warned them of the coming punishment. Christ is warning you too. There is a place of eternal punishment. Instead of going there, let Him save you!

Other New Testament passages at least infer eternal punishment: Matt. 8:12; 13:50; 22:13; 24:51; Luke 13:28; Rev. 19:20; 21:8.

Eternal Punishment in the Old Testament

The existence of eternal punishment is taught in the Old Testament as well.

"And many of them that sleep in the dust of the earth shall awake, some to everlasting life, and some to **shame and everlasting contempt**" (Dan. 12:2).

Hades, and How to Avoid Going There

Many Jehovah's Witnesses also object that hades is not a place of eternal punishment because the dead do not remain there forever, but are taken out to be judged. It is true that they are taken out to be judged, but read the passage which says this, and notice what happens next.

> "...and death and hell delivered up the dead which were in them: and they were judged every man according to their works. And death and hell were cast into the lake of fire. This is the second death" (Rev. 20:13-14).

After judgment, they will be thrown into the lake of fire. What will happen in this lake had just been described in 20:10: **"...shall be tormented day and night for ever and ever."**

The next verse (Rev. 20:15) specifies who will be saved and who will not: "And whosoever was not found written in the book of life was cast into the lake of fire." Not one of those judged for their works will be saved. The saved are those written in the book of life, those that Christ saved. To make this clear, this book is also called the Lamb's book of life in Rev. 13:8 and 21:27. (This is less obvious in the New World Translation because the same Greek word is translated "book" in Rev. 20:15 and "scroll" in the other two verses).

There is a place of eternal punishment, and whether you go there or not depends on whether you choose to trust Christ who saves, or religious teachers who give greater importance to a person's own works. If you trust in Christ, your name too will be written in the book of life of the lamb of God who was sacrificed to satisfy God's judgment on sin.

God knew we would not live a sinless life, and provided for our salvation in a way that did not compromise His righteousness:

> "For all have sinned, …being justified freely by his grace through the redemption that is in Christ Jesus whom God hath set forth to be a propitiation through faith in his blood, to declare his righteousness for the remission of sins that are past, …that he might be just, and the justifier of him which believeth in Jesus" (Rom. 3:23-26).

Please read the entire passage together with the verses before and after. The Bible also puts it this way:

> "And this is the record, that **God hath given to us eternal life, and this life is in his Son. He that hath the Son hath life; and he that hath not the Son of God hath not life"** (1 John 5:11-12).

The choice is between everlasting life, and everlasting punishment. We have all sinned and deserve to be punished, but Christ gives us the most important invitation anyone ever had:

> **"I am the door: by me if any man enter in, he shall be saved…** The thief cometh not, but for to steal, and to kill, and to destroy: **I am come that they might have life, and that they might have it more abundantly"** (John 10:9-10).

Please accept this wonderful offer.

the earth (Matt. 5:5). They explained, "The saved will not go to heaven, but will inherit the earth after death." Only after he left, when I read the whole passage, did I realize that just two verses earlier Christ had said, "Happy are those conscious of their spiritual need, since the kingdom of the heavens belongs to them" (Matt. 5:3). Following the verse he had shown me was verse ten which was very similar, and after that, verse 12 says if you are persecuted "your reward is great in the heavens…"

Obviously the verse they pointed out to me should not be interpreted in a way that would contradict the rest of the passage which teaches that our reward is in fact in heaven. Reading the whole passage, it was obvious that the overall teaching of the passage is that the saved do go to heaven. While inheriting land could be taken in a sense that would contradict the rest of the passage, it should be interpreted to go with the passage, that is, the mild tempered ones inherit land during their life time. If I had not read the verses before and after the one these teachers presented to me, I may well have believed their statement that the saved don't go to heaven. One verse, taken out of context, had been cleverly used to teach me the opposite of what the whole passage clearly said.

Interpret the Unclear in the Light of the Clear

Some verses are just plain hard to understand. They should not be made to contradict the clear teaching of the majority of Scripture.

The rule is: Interpret difficult passages in the light of the clear ones. This is particularly important when unclear passages in the Old Testament, written in a particular moment of history before Christ came, are used to contradict clear passages in the New Testament, written much more specifically for our time. Obviously when the Old Testament passage tells of something that will happen in a later age, this needs to be taken into account, but the principle: "Interpret the unclear in the light of the clear," stands.

Figurative Language

Usually, the Bible lets it be known when it is speaking in a figurative sense. Otherwise, accept the literal meaning. As an example, it is usually not correct to interpret the words "Sons of Israel" to mean Englishmen, Christians, or Jehovah's Witnesses.

Real figures of speech will stand for something similar to the figure, not in opposition to it. You should not believe that "eternal punishment" means "ceasing to exist," no matter how convincing a teacher may be.

For unto us a child is born, unto us a son is given: and the government shall be upon his shoulder: and his name shall be called Wonderful, Counselor, The mighty God, The everlasting Father, The Prince of Peace.   Isaiah 9:6

6

Jesus Christ

The Lord Jesus Christ is the great subject of the Bible. He said:

"Search the scriptures; for in them ye think ye have eternal life: and they are they which testify of me, and ye will not come to me, that ye might have life"   (John 5:39-40).

The Scriptures tell us so much about Christ, because of who He is, and because it is only by faith in Him that we can be born again into God's family.

"But as many as received him, to them gave he power to become the sons of God, even to them that believe on his name which were born, not of blood, nor of the will of the flesh, nor of the will of man, but of God"   (John 1:12-13).

Many people have the wrong idea of who Christ is and why He came to earth. This keeps them from really knowing, not only Jesus Christ, but the Father as well. While He was on earth, Jesus answered some of them:

> "Ye neither know me, nor my Father: **if ye had known me, ye should have known my Father also**" (John 8:19).

They had accepted the viewpoint of their religious leaders regarding Christ, but a different Jesus Christ could not save then, and can not save now either. Compare your religion's view of Christ to that of God's word. Be sure your own faith is in the real Christ of the Bible. Your eternal destiny depends on it.

> "He that believeth on the Son hath everlasting life: and he that believeth not the Son shall not see life; but the wrath of God abideth on him" (John 3:36).

Now let's look at some important passages that teach that Christ is not only a human being, but is also God.

Is Jesus Christ God?

The official Jehovah's Witness position is that Jesus Christ is not God. Unfortunately the wording of some passages in the New World Translation has been based on this opinion rather than on the actual words of the original.

Whenever you notice a significant difference in the New World Translation, check it with a number of other translations. You will notice that the Bible teaches that Christ is God who took on human nature to live among men.

Christ is called God in the New Testament

"But unto the Son he saith, 'Thy throne, O God, is for ever and ever: a sceptre of righteousness is the sceptre of thy kingdom" (Heb. 1:8).

In context, this verse is clearly speaking of Christ and calling him God. It quotes Psalm 45:6, an Old Testament prophesy of Christ: **"Thy throne, O God, is for ever and ever:** the sceptre of thy kingdom is a right sceptre". Jesus Christ continued to be God even after He had also taken upon Himself human nature at the virgin birth. It is His kingdom you are trying to enter. The scepter stood for the king's authority. Christ holds the sceptre, and you may only enter His kingdom in the way that He provides (See Matt. 22:8-14).

"And the Word was God"

John 1:1 is very important because it not only identifies Christ as God, but the verses that follow attribute the creation to Him:

"In the beginning was the Word, and the Word was with God, and the Word was God. The same was in the beginning with God. All things were made by him; and without him was not any thing made that was made" (John 1:1-3).

The New World Translation of the Jehovah's Witnesses says: "…and the Word was **a god,**" contrary to all other translations I have ever seen. Their officials say that this translation is justified because in the original Greek the word "God" is without the article. It is without the article, but it is clear that this is not their real reason, because verses 6, 12, and 13, of the same first chapter of John contain similar usages of the word "God," all without the article. The Witnesses have translated all of these correctly with a capital "G" and without inserting "a". The only instances I have found in which they translate "God" with a small "g" are when "God" refers to Christ. It is certainly not done consistently whenever the Greek word "God" lacks the article. (See the examples in John 3:21, 8:54, 9:16, 9:33). In the case of John 1:1-3, to avoid a translation that correctly identifies Christ as God, the New World Translation ends up attributing the creation of all things to "a god!"

Does "a god" Equal "Jehovah?"

I have found one contradiction to the claim that the lack of the article before "God" in the Greek requires the translation "a god" in English that I find particularly striking. The New World translates the very same word for "God," without an article: "…they will all be taught by **Jehovah**" (John 6:45). Why didn't they follow what they say is their rule and translate it, "They will all be taught by a god?" Because John 6:45 quotes

the Old Testament where the Hebrew word used for
God is "Jehovah" (Isa. 54:13)! *See there versions*

Why Does the Bible Call Christ
Both God and Man?

The explanation is found in John 1:14.

"And **the Word was made flesh** and dwelt among
us and we beheld his glory, the glory as of the only
begotten of the Father, full of grace and truth."

Christ, who has always been God, was made flesh at His
birth so He could live with people and be sacrificed for them.
That's why he was born of the virgin Mary and called
Emmanuel which means, "God with us" (Matt. 1:23).

Christ and the Father Are One

Paul demonstrates the fact that Jesus Christ was God as
well as man as he looks forward to Christ's return in Titus
2:13-14: "Expecting the blessed hope and appearance of
the glory **of the great God and Savior of us, Christ
Jesus** who gave himself for us that he might ransom us
from all lawlessness…" (Word for word translation from
the Greek).

When Philip asked, "Lord, show us the Father," Jesus
answered: "He that hath seen me hath seen the Father…"
(John 14:8-9). Christ is again called God in John 20:28-29
when Thomas had just seen His resurrected body:

"And Thomas answered and said unto him, **My**

Lord and my God. Jesus saith unto him, Thomas, because thou hast seen me, thou hast believed: **blessed are they that have not seen, and yet have believed."**

Would you like to be blessed? Believe what Thomas believed! The blood of Christ was God's own blood: "…the church of God, which he hath purchased with his own blood" (Acts 20:28). See also Rom. 9:5; Col. 2:9; Titus 2:13, Phlp. 2:5-11.

The Words "God" and "Christ" Are Used Interchangeably

"But ye are not in the flesh, but in the Spirit, if so be that the **Spirit of God** dwell in you. Now if any man have not the **Spirit of Christ,** he is none of his" (Rom. 8:9).

The same Holy Spirit is both Christ's Spirit, and God's Spirit. Do you have the Spirit of Christ? He will come into your heart too when you are born of the Spirit (John 3:3-7, 14-18).

"Lord of lords and King of kings"

"…and the Lamb shall overcome them: for he is Lord of lords, and King of kings" (Rev. 17:14).

This passage should clear up any lingering question as to whether or not Christ is an inferior "god". It clearly states that He is God over all (See also Rev. 19:13,16).

Christ's Works

"Jesus answered them, I told you, and ye believed not: **the works that I do in my Father's name, they bear witness of me,** but ye believe not, because ye are not of my sheep" (John 10:25-26).

The reason that many do not believe in Christ is not because proof is lacking, but because they are not His sheep. Don't despair, though, if you believe, but find that your faith wavers on occasion. When John the Baptist was thrown into prison, even he doubted, and sent messengers to ask Christ if He were the one who was to come. Christ's answer was in essence, "You will know if you look at my works." He said:

"...the blind see, the lame walk, the lepers are cleansed, the deaf hear, the dead are raised, to the poor the gospel is preached" (Luke 7:22).

If, however, you firmly believe that Christ was not God, and want to convince others of that viewpoint, prove it to them. Show them you don't have to be God to do the works which Christ did. Do them yourself!

Before Jesus raised Lazarus from the dead, He said:

"I am the resurrection, and the life: he that believeth in me, though he were dead, yet shall he live" (John 11:25).

On another occasion, Christ said to a paralytic, "Son, thy sins be forgiven thee," and some of those who heard said, "Who can forgive sins but God only?" Christ then healed the man who had been paralyzed. Doing it this way, they saw who

He was and could figure out for themselves why He could forgive sins (Mark 2:5,7).

Many reject Christ as God and Savior and claim that our salvation depends on our works. How would you answer the question: "Can Christ forgive sins and give life to the dead or are our own accomplishments necessary also?" Christ the Savior claimed to save and proved what He claimed. What proof do those offer who don't believe, and assign works for us to accomplish to earn our own salvation?

The Old Testament Foretold Christ's Divinity

"Therefore the Lord himself shall give you a sign; Behold, a virgin shall conceive, and bear a son, and shall call his name Immanuel" (Isa. 7:14).

The meaning of this prophecy was explained to Joseph by an angel just before Christ's birth:

"Behold, a virgin shall be with child, and shall bring forth a son, and they shall call his name Emmanuel, which being interpreted is, **God with us**" (Matt. 1:23).

Christ was God dwelling with man. Another important prophecy in which Christ is very clearly called God is, Isaiah 9:6:

"For unto us a child is born, unto us **a son is given:** and the government shall be upon his shoulder: and **his name shall be called Wonderful, Counselor, The mighty God,** The everlasting Father, The Prince of Peace."

In this verse the New World Translation emphasizes Christ's divinity with another capitol letter, calling him "Mighty God".

Both Christ and His Father Were Called "I Am"

God said His name was I am:

"And God said unto Moses, **I AM THAT I AM:** and he said, Thus shalt thou say unto the children of Israel, **I AM hath sent me unto you. . . this is my name for ever...**" (Ex. 3:14-15).

Jesus also applied the name "I am" to Himself and the Jews recognized that He was claiming to be God. Since they did not believe that He was, they tried to kill him:

"Thou art not yet fifty years old, and hast thou seen Abraham? ...Before Abraham was, I am. Then took they up stones to cast at him..." (John 8:57-59).

Will you believe Christ, or treat Him like a liar and blasphemer?

Jesus Christ is Jehovah

• Jehovah said: "...and they shall look upon **me whom they have pierced**" (Zec. 12:10). The preceding verses (1, 4, 7, 8) identify Jehovah as the one speaking. Christ is the one who was pierced, and John 19:37 clearly tells us that this prophecy was fulfilled in His crucifixion.

• Jeremiah the prophet predicted that God would raise

up a descendent of David who would reign and be called
LORD, or Jehovah: "...this is his name whereby he shall
be called, THE LORD (Jehovah) OUR RIGHTEOUS-
NESS" (Jer. 23:6). Jesus Christ was the descendent of
David, who was to be called Jehovah our righteousness.

• Who is Lord of the Sabbath? Christ said that He is.
"Therefore the Son of man is Lord also of the sabbath"
(Mark 2:28).

Only One Can Be the First and the Last. That One Is Called Both Jesus and Jehovah!

"Thus saith **the LORD** the King of Israel, **and his
redeemer the LORD of hosts; I** am the **first,** and
I am the **last;** and beside me there is no God"
(Isa. 44:6).

The Redeemer is, throughout the New Testament, identified as Christ Jesus. In this Scripture He is called LORD
(Jehovah). It is clear in this passage that the title "the first
and the last" belongs to Jehovah the Redeemer. Look
where this title is repeated!

Two Pairs of Passages in Revelation

God makes the identification of Christ with Jehovah
even more clear and undeniable in two pairs of passages in
Revelation which speak of the first and the last. Only one
can be first. There can be no second first. The "last" is
also exclusive.

The First Pair Is in Chapter One

The one who is coming in these verses is Jesus Christ, the one who was pierced, who is also clearly called "Jehovah God":

- "Behold, he cometh with clouds; and every eye shall see him, and they also which pierced him: and all kindred of the earth shall wail because of him. Even so, Amen. I am Alpha and Omega, the beginning and the ending, saith the Lord, which is, and which was, and which is to come, the Almighty" (Rev. 1:7-8).

To make it more clear that the Jesus who was pierced and is coming with the clouds is Jehovah, here is the same passage from the New World Translation:

"Look! He is coming with the clouds, and **every eye will see him,** and those who pierced him; and all the tribes of the earth will beat themselves in grief because of him. Yes, Amen. **'I am the Alpha and the Omega,' says Jehovah God, 'the One** who is and who was and who is coming, the Almighty'" (Rev. 1:7-8).

This identification becomes even more clear in the second verse of this pair where Jesus Christ, the one who died, is identified as Jehovah by calling Him the First and the Last, the exact same words which we saw used for Jehovah a few paragraphs above in the quote from Isaiah 44:6. So you can compare the verses more easily, here is that quote again, this time from the New World Translation: "This is what Jehovah has said, the King of Israel and the Repurchaser of him, Jehovah of armies, 'I am the first and I am the last, and besides me there is no God'". Here is the second of the pair of verses in Revelation:

* "…I am the **first** and the **last:** I am he that liveth, and was dead; and, behold, I am alive for evermore…" To make even more clear that Jehovah is the one who was dead and now lives, the New World Translation capitalizes "First" and "Last". Here it is: "I am the **First** and the **Last,** and the living one; and **I became dead, but, look! I am living** forever and ever…" (Rev. 1:17-18). Jehovah is called the one who died and is living which is Jesus Christ.

The Second Pair Is in Chapters 21-22

* "And he that sat upon the throne said, Behold, I make all things new. And he said unto me, Write: for these words are true and faithful. And he said unto me, It is done. I am **Alpha** and **Omega, the beginning and the end.** I will give unto him that is athirst of the fountain of the water of life freely. He that overcometh shall inherit all things; and **I will be his God,** and he shall be my son" (Rev. 21:5-7).

In this passage the Alpha and the Omega, the beginning and the end is God, the one seated on the throne, but in the second of this pair Christ the one who is coming quickly is the Alpha and the Omega, the beginning and the end.

* "Behold, **I come quickly… I am Alpha and Omega, the beginning and the end, the first and the last"** (Rev. 22:12, 13).

Not only are the same words used of Christ in 22:13 that were used of the one sitting on the throne in 21:5-7, but He is also called "the **first** and the **last,**" again applying the description of Jehovah in Isaiah to Christ: "I am the first and I am the last, and besides me there is no God" (Isa. 44:6).

If you are thinking, "Can I believe that this is Christ, when it is Jehovah?" Yes, you can, because as the passage continues, It says:

* **"I, Jesus…"** (Rev. 22:16).

The one who is "coming quickly" (22:13) is also identified:

* "Surely I come quickly. Amen. Even so, come, Lord Jesus." (Rev. 22:20).

There can not logically be two beginnings and two ends. There aren't, the Lord Jesus Christ is Jehovah, come in human flesh.

John the Baptist Prepared the Way of Jehovah

John the Baptist explained why he was preparing the way for Jesus Christ by quoting the words of Isaiah, "Prepare ye the way of the **LORD,** make straight in the desert a highway for our **God**" (Isa. 40:3). The *New World Translation* of the Jehovah's Witnesses puts it, "Clear up the way of **Jehovah…**"

Matthew shows how John fulfilled this prophecy by preparing the way of Jesus Christ (3:3, 11-17).

The book of Mark begins with the announcement that God was sending John the Baptist to prepare the way of Jesus Christ saying, "Prepare ye the way of the Lord, make his paths straight" (Mark 1:1-3). The New World Translation: "Prepare the way **of Jehovah,** you people, make his roads straight…" John the Baptist, in preparing the way of Christ fulfilled this prophecy. He prepared the way of Jehovah because Jehovah is Jesus Christ come in the flesh.

Luke's Gospel says that at John the Baptist's birth, his father had prophesied that John would make Jehovah's ways ready: "And thou, child, shalt be called the prophet of the Highest: for thou shalt go before the face of the Lord to prepare his ways" (Luke 1:76). New World: "…you will go in advance **before Jehovah** to make his ways ready". John made Jehovah's ways ready by preparing the way of Christ (Luke 3:4, 16).

In the first chapter of John's Gospel, when people asked John, "who are you?" he answered: "I am the voice of one crying in the wilderness, Make straight the way of the Lord, as said the prophet Esaias" (John 1:23. See Isa. 40:3). New World: "…Make the way of **Jehovah** straight…" Lets pick up the narrative three verses ahead, and see who it is talking about.

> "John answered them, saying, I baptize with water: but there standeth one among you, whom ye know not. He it is, who coming after me is preferred before me, whose shoe's latchet I am not worthy to unloose… The next day John seeth Jesus coming unto him, and saith, Behold the Lamb of God, which taketh away the sin of the world… I knew him not: but that he should be made manifest to Israel, therefore am I come baptizing with water" (John 1:26-27, 29, 31).

For whom was John preparing the way? For Jehovah. That is why John was not worthy to untie His sandal, but John also called Him "Jesus" and "the Lamb of God that takes away the sin of the world," and said that the reason he had come was to make Him manifest to Israel. Just four verses ahead, John again identifies the Lamb of God whose way he was making straight:

> "Again the next day John was standing with two of his disciples, and as he looked at Jesus walking he said: **'See, the Lamb of God!'"** (John 1:35).

God the Son existed with the Father before John was born. Then He came and was born here on earth so that we might know God. That's why He was called Immanuel, God with us (Matt. 1:23), and why John prepared the way for Jesus when he prepared the way for Jehovah (See also Php. 2:5-8).

There Is Only One Savior: Jehovah
This One Savior Is also Called Jesus

"I, even I, am the LORD; and beside me there is no saviour" (Isa. 43:11). See also Hos. 13:4; Jude 1:25; Titus 3:4-7. The New World Translation puts it: **"I—I am Jehovah, and besides me there is no Savior".**

• "For unto you is born this day in the city of David a Saviour, which is Christ the Lord" (Luke 2:11).

• Speaking of Christ, Acts 4:12 says: "Neither is there salvation in any other: for there is none other name under heaven given among men, whereby we must be saved" (See also Titus 2:13, 2 Pet. 3:18).

- "But is now made manifest by the appearing of our Saviour Jesus Christ, who hath abolished death, and hath brought life and immortality to light through the gospel" (2 Tim. 1:10).
- "For so an entrance shall be ministered unto you abundantly into the everlasting kingdom of our Lord and Saviour Jesus Christ" (2 Pet. 1:11).

If you could do enough works to save yourself, you and Christ would both be saviors, but Christ and Jehovah are one Savior.

Arguments to the Contrary

To deny the divine nature of Jesus, the Watchtower shows his human nature and that he has the relationship of Son to the Father. He does, but before He took on the human nature, He already had the divine nature. "...And the Word was made flesh, and dwelt among us" (John 1:14) when He, "made himself of no reputation, and took upon him the form of a servant, and was made in the likeness of men" (Php. 2:7), He already had the divine nature. He humbled Himself to take on a human nature as well when He was born of the virgin and called "God with us".

Whose Witnesses Should We Be?

We are not told to be Jehovah's witnesses in some generic way, but it is specified that we should be witnesses of Jesus Christ:

- "But ye shall receive power, after that the Holy

Ghost is come upon you: and ye shall be witnesses unto me both in Jerusalem, and in all Judaea, and in Samaria, and unto the uttermost part of the earth" (Acts 1:8).

• "And he commanded us to preach unto the people, and **to testify that it is he which was ordained of God to be the Judge of quick and dead.** To him give all the prophets witness, that **through his name whosoever believeth in him shall receive remission of sins"** (Acts 10:42-43).

The apostles did as they were told, and went out as witnesses of Jesus Christ: "And with great power **gave the apostles witness of the resurrection of the Lord Jesus…"** (Acts 4:33).

Even the Holy Spirit was a witness of Christ. Peter and the other apostles, when they had told of Christ's death and resurrection and that He forgives sins said, "And we are his witnesses of these things; and so is also the Holy Ghost, whom God hath given to them that obey him. When they heard that, they were cut to the heart, and took counsel to slay them" (Acts 5:32). Which side are you on? Would you prefer that Christ's witnesses were done away with, or would you like to join them in their witness that Jesus Christ is that one Savior?

...₃ answered and said unto them, Destroy this temple, and in three days I will raise it up. Then said the Jews, Forty and six years was this temple in building, and wilt thou rear it up in three days? But he spake of the temple of his body. John 2:19-21

7

The Resurrection of Jesus

Jehovah's Witnesses teach that Jesus was resurrected, but "as a spirit creature." More specifically, they teach that at the resurrection, His body stayed dead but the tomb became empty because God hid Christ's body somewhere else.

Jesus Christ Stated That He Would Raise His Body

Note the contrast between Christ's teaching that He would raise His body, and the doctrine of the Jehovah's Witnesses:

"Jesus answered and said unto them, Destroy this temple, and **in three days I will raise it up.** Then said the Jews, Forty and six years was this temple in building, and wilt thou rear it up in three days? But **he spake of the temple of his**

body. When therefore he was risen from the dead, his disciples remembered that he had said this unto them; and they believed the scripture, and the word which Jesus had said" (John 2:19-22).

Christ's prophecy here was that He would raise His body. Would it have caused the disciples to believe if Jesus' prophecy had been wrong, and He had not raised His body but only His Spirit?

Your choice is clear. Believe the powerful teaching of the Bible that Christ would and did raise His body, or the weak reasoning of men who say He didn't!

Had Christ not been raised in the way that He said he would, a good time to explain what really happened would have been when the women went to the grave, found it empty and saw an angel who explained: "...He is not here, for he was raised up, as he said. Come see the place where he was lying." Why did the angel say, "He was raised up, as he said" if He had not been raised up as He said?

It would have been the perfect time to explain, "He was raised up spiritually, then God took His dead body and hid it." The anti-Biblical doctrine that Christ's body was not raised from the dead, but was taken and hidden originated in the minds of men and contradicts the Word of Jehovah.

For Old Testament prophecies that teach that Christ would be raised from the dead, see Psalm 16:10 and Isaiah 53:10-12. Read both in the Authorized Version.

After the Resurrection, Jesus Claimed that His Body Had Been Raised and Proved it

The disciples had a tendency to believe in ghosts, that is, spirits that at times materialized bodies so people could see them. Earlier, when they saw Christ walk on water, the disciples thought they had seen a ghost (Matt. 14:26; Mark 6:49). Since He knew they were thinking this again, He went out of His way to prove that this was really His body:

> "But they were terrified and affrighted, and supposed that they had seen a spirit. And he said unto them, Why are ye troubled? and why do thoughts arise in your hearts? Behold my hands and my feet, that it is I myself: handle me, and see; for a spirit hath not flesh and bones, as ye see me have. And when he had thus spoken, he shewed them his hands and his feet. And while they yet believed not for joy, and wondered, he said unto them, Have ye here any meat? And they gave him a piece of a broiled fish, and of an honeycomb. And he took it, and did eat before them" (Luke 24:37-43).

Note that Jesus first said: "It is I myself," and then proved that He had real flesh and bones.

When people who were not there contradict this and say the disciples saw a spirit creature, you must decide whether to believe their word, or the Word of Jehovah.

Though at first it seemed too good to be true, after

seeing and feeling Christ's body, with the wounds in His hands and feet, the disciples believed, and "returned to Jerusalem with great joy" (Luke 24:52). When they thought they were seeing a spirit they were "frightened" and "troubled". When they knew it was Christ Himself; that He had flesh and bones and could eat, they experienced "great joy." The joy of believing in Christ's resurrection is a joy which you can and should share.

Thomas was not present when Jesus showed the disciples his resurrected body, and he did not believe their testimony. In fact, he told those who had been present that he would not believe unless he could touch the wounds. Jesus visited the disciples again and what he told Thomas will help you too:

> "Then saith he to Thomas, Reach hither thy finger, and behold my hands; and reach hither thy hand, and thrust it into my side: and be not faithless, but believing. And Thomas answered and said unto him, My Lord and my God. Jesus saith unto him, Thomas, because thou hast seen me, thou hast believed: blessed are they that have not seen, and yet have believed" (John 20:27-29).

Seeing and touching Christ's body with the wounds convinced Thomas, but through this Scripture, Jesus is also talking to you, "Happy are those who do not see and yet believe." Are you skeptical? Don't assume that Jesus must be wrong because His words contradict what you have been told by people you respect. Put

Him to the test! Believe that He is your Lord and your God, who really rose from the dead. "Blessed are they that have not seen, and yet have believed."

WHAT is your Witness

What Should Our Witness Be?

We saw in the previous chapter that those who follow God in New Testament times are to be Christ's witnesses. Now we will see that our witness about Christ is to focus on His death for sins, and particularly on His resurrection, because His death and resurrection are crucial to salvation.

Before He returned into heaven, Jesus said:

> "...thus it behoved Christ to suffer, and to rise from the dead the third day: And that repentance and remission of sins should be preached in his name among all nations, beginning at Jerusalem. And ye are witnesses of these things" (Luke 24:46-47).

Are you a witness to others of the power of Christ's death and resurrection to bring forgiveness for sins?

What Was the Witness of the Apostles?

An example of Peter's witness is found in a sermon of his which is recorded in Acts 2. He quotes Psalm 16:8-10, explaining that it is speaking of Jesus (Read it in the AV). He gets to the point in Acts 2:27 where the Psalm he is quoting says of Christ:

"Because thou wilt not leave my soul in hell, neither wilt thou suffer thine Holy One to see corruption."

Peter goes on to explain that David:

"He seeing this before spake of the resurrection of Christ, that his soul was not left in hell, neither his flesh did see corruption. This Jesus hath God raised up, whereof we all are witnesses" (Acts 2:31-32).

Peter said that Jesus's flesh did not see corruption; just what had been prophesied in the Old Testament.

All of those first believers gave witnesses to this, as should each one who follows Jehovah and believes His word. Do not be deceived, Christ's resurrection was not just spiritual, nor was his body hidden like that of Moses in some other place where, baring a miracle, it would "see corruption". The men that teach that God hid the body must either say that His body did see corruption, or make up a whole new kind of miracle, the perpetual conservation of the body. Why should we reject the Biblical miracle of the resurrection to make up a harder one? Our testimony should be the uncorrupted one given by the Apostles. "And with great power gave the apostles witness of the resurrection of the Lord Jesus (Acts 4:33). See also Acts 3:14-15; 5:30-32, 10:40-41, 1 Cor. 15:1-4.

Your Salvation Depends on Christ's Resurrection

• "And if Christ be not raised, your faith is vain; ye are yet in your sins" (1 Cor. 15:17, see also 1 Cor. 15:16-21, Col. 2:12-13).

• "Moreover, brethren, I declare unto you the gospel... by which also ye are saved, how that Christ died for our sins according to the scriptures; and that he was buried, and that he rose again the third day according to the scriptures" (1 Cor. 15:1-4).

Having seen that your salvation depends on your believing that Christ died, and was raised again according to the Scriptures, you are ready for Acts 13:32-39, a passage similar to that which we have already read in Acts 2. Please read the whole passage from your Bible as I only have room to quote parts of it:

• "And we declare unto you glad tidings, how that the promise which was made unto the fathers, God hath fulfilled the same unto us their children, in that he hath raised up Jesus... no more to return to corruption... Thou shalt not suffer thine Holy One to see corruption... But he, whom God raised again, saw no corruption... through this man is preached unto you the forgiveness of sins, And by him all that believe are justified from all things, from which ye could not be justified by the law of Moses."

You can either believe God's word and be declared guiltless, or believe someone else's ideas that are contrary to the Scriptures and try to save yourself in some other way, but you will not really be saved unless you believe in the real Christ who died for your sins and rose from the dead, body and spirit.

"...And if Christ be not raised, your faith is vain;
ye are yet in your sins" (1 Cor. 15:17).

The good news is, Christ has been raised up and the resurrected Christ saves those who trust in Him. Why not trust Him to save you now? Why risk remaining another minute in your sins?

Arguments to the Contrary

To uphold the theory that Christ's body was not resurrected, some quote a few passages which can be understood in more than one way. One says, "...flesh and blood cannot inherit the kingdom of God; neither doth corruption inherit incorruption." The passage continues however, "We shall not all sleep, but we shall all be changed... For this corruptible must put on incorruption..." (1 Cor. 15:50-53). Changed! Our corruptible body will put on incorruptibility. The verse does not even infer that Christ's body was substituted with a new materialized one, or that that might be our fate. The body will be changed, putting on incorruptibility. It will not be substituted with a materialized body as might seem to be the case if one stopped reading before verse 53. Always read the whole passage.

Some also quote:

> "For Christ also hath once suffered for sins, the just for the unjust, that he might bring us to God, being put to death in the flesh, but quickened by the Spirit: By which also he went and preached unto the spirits in prison" (1 Pet. 3:18-19).

This passage has been used to teach that after the

resurrection, Christ was alive only spiritually. While the New World Translation says that Christ was made alive "in the spirit," others use the equally good translation "by the Spirit" which says nothing about the state of His body one way or the other.

However, it is the timing which is important! When was it that He preached to the spirits in prison? Most probably it occurred while his body was in the tomb, rather than after his resurrection. In fact, a few verses ahead, the passage speaks of where He went after the resurrection and ascension: "He is at God's right hand for he went his way to heaven..." (1 Pet. 3:22).

How Did Christ Raise Others?

The idea that the Lord Jesus Christ's body was taken away by God to be buried like that of Moses is a completely man made doctrine without any Biblical basis whatsoever. It not only contradicts the many passages which we have just quoted, but is also highly unlikely when one remembers the others that Christ raised. Lazarus and all the rest were raised physically. Christ never raised anyone just spiritually as the Watchtower says that He Himself was raised (John 11-43-44; Matt. 9:25; Luke 7:14-15).

How Can Your Body Be Raised?

"But if the Spirit of him that raised up Jesus from the dead dwell in you, he that raised up

Christ from the dead shall also quicken your mortal bodies by his Spirit that dwelleth in you" (Rom. 8:11).

By the reasoning of the Jehovah's Witnesses, many of the people who first received this letter would have been included in the 144,000. Since they were able to live in heaven with resurrected bodies, the line of reasoning that says that Christ could not is obviously false.

If you trust Christ as Savior and receive His Spirit, when you die, your mortal body will be made alive like that of Jesus.

Jehovah's Witness Leaders Believe in Bodily Resurrection

You will remember from chapter two that the Jehovah's Witness leaders strongly believed: "...the faithful men of old will soon be resurrected by the Lord on the earth, and take charge of the visible affairs of earth." As a testimony to this faith, they built a house around 1929 for the Old Testament patriarchs to live in when they returned to earth. (See the quote at the end of chapter two). They built the house despite the fact that the Watchtower Society had been wrong previously when they had predicted that the return of the Old Testament faithful would occur in 1914, 1915, 1918 and 1925.

Spirits don't need houses! Bodies need houses! The

leaders of the Watchtower Society built a house because they knew God raises people's bodies. They believed the "faithful men of old," would be resurrected with their bodies. But at the same time they refused to admit this about Christ, in spite of the clear teaching of the word of Jehovah:

> "...that Christ died for our sins according to the scriptures; and that he was buried, and that he rose again the third day according to the scriptures" (1 Cor. 15:3-4).

Know ye not that ye are the temple of God,
and that the Spirit of God dwelleth in you?
1 Corinthians 3:16

8

The Holy Spirit

The Jehovah's Witnesses believe: "The holy spirit is not a person; it is God's active force."[1]

Since they do not believe that the Holy Spirit is either a person, or God, but just a force, they do not write "Holy Spirit" with capital letters, even when translating Scripture. Other translators consider Him God, and capitalize. This has become proper English usage, as a glance at a dictionary will show.

After reading the passages that touch on this, I believe you will agree that the Holy Spirit stands out both as a divine person, and as God. Lets notice first that His actions are not just those of a force, but that He does things that only a person can do. After that we will examine His divinity.

[1]Watchtower, Official Web Site of Jehovah's Witnesses.

The Holy Spirit Is a Person, Not Just a Force

He Does All the Things That Distinguish a Person from a Force

A force pushes or pulls or otherwise exerts pressure. People can exert force, but so can water, wind and gravity. People have many other abilities that forces don't have. The following are some of them. Other than the titles, I give almost no comment. May the Scriptures themselves speak to your heart as you interpret them for yourself.

Forces Don't Know and Teach, The Spirit Does

• "But God hath revealed them unto us by his Spirit: for the Spirit searcheth all things, yea, the deep things of God. For what man knoweth the things of a man, save the spirit of man which is in him? even so the things of God knoweth no man, but the Spirit of God. Now we have received, not the spirit of the world, but the spirit which is of God; that we might know the things that are freely given to us of God. Which things also we speak, not in the words which man's wisdom teacheth, but which the Holy Ghost teacheth..." (1 Cor. 2:11-12).

• "For the Holy Ghost shall teach you in the same hour what ye ought to say" (Luke 12:12, See also 1 Cor. 2:10, 13; John 14:26).

The Spirit Has Emotions, Forces Don't

• **He loves:** "Now I beseech you, brethren, for the Lord Jesus Christ's sake, and for the love of the Spirit..." (Rom. 15:30).

• **He can be grieved:** "And grieve not the holy Spirit

of God, whereby ye are sealed unto the day of redemption" (Eph. 4:30).

• **He can be insulted:** "…and hath done despite unto the Spirit of grace" (Heb. 10:29).

The Spirit Speaks

• "He that hath an ear, let him hear what the Spirit saith unto the churches…" (Rev. 2:7, See also: Rev. 2:11,17; 3:6, 13, 22; Acts 1:16; 8:29; 10:19; 11:12; 2 Pet. 1:21).

• **He speaks in the first person:** "…Well spake the Holy Ghost by Esaias the prophet unto our fathers saying… and I should heal them" (Acts 28:25-27).

• **Can a force speak of the future?:** "…which the Holy Ghost by the mouth of David spake before concerning Judas…" (Acts 1:16, See also 20:23, John 16:13-14).

• **He testifies:** "But when the Comforter is come, whom I will send unto you from the Father, even the Spirit of truth, which proceedeth from the Father, he shall testify of me" (John 15:26).

The Spirit Gave the Ability to Speak in Foreign Languages

"And they were all filled with the Holy Ghost, and began to speak with other tongues, as the Spirit gave them utterance" (Acts 2:4).

The Spirit Guides

• "Howbeit when he, the Spirit of truth, is come, he will guide you into all truth…" (John 16:13).

• "For as many as are led by the Spirit of God, they are the sons of God" (Rom. 8:14).

The Spirit Ordains

• **He sends out missionaries:** "…the Holy Ghost said, Separate me Barnabas and Saul for the work whereunto I have called them. So they, being sent forth by the Holy Ghost, departed unto Seleucia" (Acts 13:2 - 4).

• **He appoints overseers:** "…Take heed therefore unto yourselves, and to all the flock, over the which the Holy Ghost hath made you overseers, to feed the church of God…" (Acts 20:28).

What Else Might a Person Do?

• **He comforts:** "But the Comforter, which is the Holy Ghost…" (John 14:26; see also 14:16-17; 15:26).

• **He helps:** "Likewise the Spirit also helpeth our infirmities" (Rom. 8:26).

• **He investigates:** "…the Spirit searcheth all things…" (1 Cor. 2:10).

• **He reveals:** "But God hath revealed them unto us by his Spirit…" (1 Cor. 2:10).

• **He intercedes:** "…the Spirit itself maketh intercession for us…" (Rom. 8:26).

• **He can be blasphemed:** "…the blasphemy against the Holy Ghost shall not be forgiven…" (Matt. 12:31).

• **It's possible to lie to him:** "Ananias, why hath Satan filled thine heart to lie to the Holy Ghost…" (Acts 5:3).

Arguments to the Contrary

Someone might answer, "It's true that the Spirit has all of the characteristics of a person, but He is still not a person because He has no body."

Remember, God the Father has no body either. If the lack of a body reduces the Holy Spirit to a force without a personality, what does it do to the Father?

The Holy Spirit is God
His Divinity is Stated

• "Now the Lord is that Spirit: and where the Spirit of the Lord is, there is liberty" (2 Cor. 3:17). Notice who the Spirit is according to the New World Translation: "Now Jehovah is the Spirit; and where the spirit of Jehovah is, there is freedom."

• "...exactly as done by Jehovah the Spirit" (2 Cor. 3:18, New World Translation).

His Divinity Is Demonstrated

The same Holy Spirit is called the Spirit of Jehovah, the Spirit of God, and the Spirit of Christ. What is done to God's Spirit is done to God Himself:

• "...Ananias, why hath Satan filled thine heart to lie to the Holy Ghost... thou hast not lied unto men, but unto God" (Acts 5:3-4).

• "Know ye not that ye are the temple of God, and that the Spirit of God dwelleth in you?" (1 Cor. 3:16).

• "And because ye are sons, God hath sent forth the Spirit of his Son into your hearts, crying, Abba, Father" (Gal. 4:6. See also Rom 8:9; 1 Pet. 1:11).

The Spirit of God Is the Spirit of Christ, and Only Those in Whom He Dwells Are Saved

"But ye are not in the flesh, but in the Spirit, if so be that the Spirit of God dwell in you. Now if any man have not the Spirit of Christ, he is none of his… But if the Spirit of him that raised up Jesus from the dead dwell in you, he that raised up Christ from the dead shall also quicken your mortal bodies by his Spirit that dwelleth in you" (Rom. 8:9,11).

The grace of the Lord Jesus Christ, and the love of God, and the communion of the Holy Ghost, be with you all. 2 Corinthians 13:14

9

The Trinity

The word "trinity" is not found in the Bible. It came into use later to describe in one word the teaching of the Scriptures that there is one God with three personalities, or as it is usually stated, "in three persons."

Though the Bible clearly assumes that this relationship exists, Jehovah's Witnesses' leaders have developed a doctrine that demotes the Holy Spirit to a force and Christ to only a man, or a god with a small "g", denying that the one God exists in three persons.

When the Bible Puts the Father, Son, and Holy Spirit on the Same Level in the Same Scripture, It Shows Us the Trinity

• "The grace of the Lord Jesus Christ, and the love of God, and the communion of the Holy Ghost, be with you all" (2 Cor. 13:14).

• "Go ye therefore, and teach all nations, baptizing them in the name of the Father, and of the Son, and of the Holy Ghost..." (Matt. 28:19). See also John 14:26, Luke 3:21-22. Since the Bible says there is only one God, we know we are not to baptize in the name of three gods, but the passage clearly speaks of three persons. "Name" in Hebrew speaks as much of the nature of the person as of what he is called. We are to baptize in the name (singular) of all three of the persons of God.

• "And because ye are sons, God hath sent forth the Spirit of his Son into your hearts, crying, Abba, Father" (Gal. 4:6).

Christ and the Father Are Not Separate Gods, They Have the Same Spirit

"But ye are not in the flesh, but in the Spirit, if so be that the Spirit of God dwell in you. Now if any man have not the Spirit of Christ, he is none of his... But if the Spirit of him that raised up Jesus from the dead dwell in you, he that raised up Christ from the dead shall also quicken your mortal bodies by his Spirit that dwelleth in you" (Rom. 8:9-11).

Here we find the same Spirit called both the Spirit of God and the Spirit of Christ. The one Spirit is the Spirit of both the Father and the Son. This shows us that they are not separate Gods. If they were, they would not have the same Spirit. In this passage we see the Father, the Son, and the Holy Spirit, the three persons of the one God, working together to raise the mortal bodies of the dead.

The Attributes (or Characteristics) of God Belong to the Father, the Son, and the Holy Spirit:

- Eternity (Psalm 90:2 AV, Mic. 5:2, Heb. 9:14)
- Omniscience (Jer. 17:10, Rev. 2:23, 1 Cor. 2:11)
- Omnipresence (Jer. 23:24, Matt. 18:20, Psalm 139:7)
- Holiness (Rev. 15:4, Acts 3;14, 1 Thess. 4:8)

The Works of God Are Likewise Attributed to All Three Persons

The creation is but one example (Psalm 102:25, Col. 1:16 AV, Job 33:4).

God Speaks in the Plural

In the Old Testament God sometimes speaks in the plural, probably indicating the Trinity:

- "And God (Elohim, a plural word) said, Let us make man in our image, after our likeness" (Gen. 1:26). See also Gen. 3:22.

- "Go to, let us go down, and there confound their language..." The New World Translation specifies who said this: "After that, Jehovah said... Let us go down and there confuse their language …" (Gen. 11:7).

• "Holy, holy, holy, is the LORD of hosts: the whole earth is full of his glory" (Isa. 6:3). "Also I heard the voice of the Lord, saying, Whom shall I send, and who will go for us" (Isa. 6:8)?

Each of the Three Persons Is God

In the chapters on Christ and the Holy Spirit, we have already shown many passages which present Jesus Christ as God and the Holy Spirit as God. Read these verses again, putting them together with the Scriptures that show the Father as God and you will see the Trinity.

O taste and see that the LORD is good. Psalm 34:8

10

The Name "Jehovah"

In the Bible, names have meanings. God is called a number of things, and each one emphasizes a particular aspect of his character: His divinity, his power, etc.

The Significance of "Jehovah"

"Jehovah" is the Hebrew name equated with "I Am." In some languages it is translated "The Eternal" because it describes His eternity and self existence. It comes from the same root as the verb "to be." It is often used when there is a close relationship between God and a person.

"I Am" and "Jehovah," Used Interchangeably

God expressed His eternity in another way when He called Himself "I am." As He was sending Moses to call His people out of Egypt, Moses asked Him:

"...when I come unto the children of Israel, and shall say unto them, The God of your fathers hath sent me unto you: and they shall say to me, what is His name? What shall I say unto them? And God said to Moses I AM THAT I AM: and he said, Thus shalt thou say unto the children of Israel, I AM hath sent me unto you" (Ex. 3:13-14).

The very next verse uses the name Jehovah:

"And God said moreover unto Moses, Thus shalt thou say unto the children of Israel, The LORD God of your fathers, the God of Abraham, the God of Isaac, and the God of Jacob, hath sent me unto you: this is my name for ever, and this is my memorial unto all generations" (Ex. 3:15).

God's name in this passage is expressed by two different Hebrew words, one is translated "I am" and the other is "Jehovah." Both are called God's name, and both express the idea that God is the eternal one.

Jesus Identified Himself with Jehovah

Jesus Christ, to identify Himself with Jehovah, applied God's name "I am" to Himself, using the Greek words "ego eimi" which mean "I am": "Verily, verily, I say unto you, Before Abraham was, I am" (John 8:58). The next verse makes it clear that the unbelieving Jews knew Christ Jesus was equating Himself with "I am," that is: "Jehovah." They thought His statement was blasphemous, so they tried to execute Him.

Old Testament Prophecies Equated Jehovah with Christ

In Zechariah 12:10, a prophecy which had already identified Jehovah as the one speaking (12:1, 4), Jehovah said:

"...and they shall look upon me whom they have pierced..."

This is a reference to the crucifixion. Who was pierced at the crucifixion? This passage calls Him Jehovah.

Jeremiah 23:6, another prophecy, says that at His second coming the righteous branch of David will be called "Jehovah our righteousness:" "...and this is his name whereby he shall be called, THE LORD OUR RIGHTEOUSNESS." "LORD" in caps is the King James Version's translation of "Jehovah" in the Hebrew. The New World Translation adds the word "is" which hides the fact that it refers to Christ, but it eliminates any possible doubt that the Hebrew name being used is "Jehovah:" "And this is his name with which he will be called, Jehovah is our righteousness."

It Is Not Wrong to Call Jehovah by His Other Names

The New Testament uses a number of names for God. Here are three examples:

• "For you must not prostrate yourself to another god, because **Jehovah, whose name is Jealous,** he is a jealous God" (Ex. 34:14, New World Translation).

• When Jesus called to God from the cross he said: "Eli, Eli, lama sabachthani? that is to say, My God, my God, why hast thou forsaken me?" (Matt. 27:46).

• When teaching the disciples to pray, Jesus said, "After this manner therefore pray ye: Our Father which art in heaven, Hallowed be thy name" (Matt. 6:9).

"Jehovah" May Be Translated

The New World Translators try to represent the sound of this name for God in Hebrew, writing "Jehovah." Many other translators of the Bible translate the Hebrew word with the English word "Lord." Representing the sound of the Hebrew word with "Jehovah" gives some idea of how the word sounded, but is not exact, because the Hebrew word begins with a letter which is sounded "I" and not "J."

Some feel it best not to translate "Jehovah" with the English word "Lord" as most English translations do, but to use "Jehovah". Is there any justification for the translation "Lord?"

The New Testament was originally written in Greek under the inspiration of God. When the word "Jehovah" is quoted from the Hebrew of the Old Testament, the Greek New Testament which we translate to get our New Testaments does not spell out the Hebrew word with Greek letters, but translates it with the Greek word "Kurios" ("Lord" in English). In this way, God lets us know that it is OK to translate "Jehovah" into other languages.

In addition, the entire Old Testament was translated

into Greek around 200 B.C. This translation, called the Septuagint, also translates the Hebrew word for "Jehovah" with the Greek word "Kurios."

Under the inspiration of God, the Greek New Testament refers to Christ with the same word, "Kurios," ("Lord") which it uses to translate "Jehovah." As an example, the entire title "Lord Jesus Christ" is found 82 times in the New Testament (See Romans 5:1). "Kurios," ("Lord") is not a specific term which always means Christ, but is also used at times for a person who is in charge.

There is at least one clamorous exception to the rule that the New World Translation always writes out "Jehovah." In this case the Witnesses themselves translate the Hebrew "Jehovah" as "Lord". Why?

The Exception, Jehovah in Psalm 34:8 Is Christ in 1 Peter 2:3

As a rule, the New World Translation always renders "Kurios" in the Greek New Testament as "Jehovah" when it refers to the Father, but "Lord" when it refers to Jesus Christ. Wherever the New Testament quotes the Old Testament, the New World translators could tell whether to use "Lord" or "Jehovah" by noticing if the Hebrew word which the New Testament quoted was "Jehovah."

In 1 Peter 2:3, however, they faced a real problem. The passage quotes Psalm 34:8: "Taste and see that Jehovah is good..." (New World Translation). In 1 Peter 2:3, they translated: "Provided you have tasted that the Lord is kind." Why did they not follow their rule and translate,

"Jehovah is kind?" Read on in 1 Peter and you will find that the passage is referring to Christ. To hide the fact that Jehovah of the Old Testament is the Lord Jesus Christ, the New World Translation broke its rule and used "Lord" in 1 Peter to translate "Jehovah" in the Old Testament passage.

What Name Is Above Every Other?

The name of Jesus Christ is "...above every other name" (Php. 2:9). This is not because a man is above Jehovah, but because Jesus Christ is Jehovah.

Conclusion

Which name you prefer to use for God is not terribly important, and depends to a large extent on which of His attributes you want to emphasize. What is important is that you become His child and enter His Kingdom. To do this, "Ye must be born again" (John 3:7). See the first and last chapters of this book to find out how.

For all the law is fulfilled in one word, even in this; Thou shalt love thy neighbour as thyself.
Galatians 5:14

11

Should We Give Blood?

The Old Testament clearly states that the Jews were not to eat meat that had not been properly bled:

> "And whatsoever man there be of the house of Israel, or of the strangers that sojourn among you, that eateth any manner of blood; I will even set my face against that soul that eateth blood, and will cut him off from among his people" (Lev. 17:10).

The Bible always prohibits eating, rather than drinking blood. The Hebrew word for "drink" is a common word, and the Bible speaks of drinking blood in other contexts (Numbers 23:24 and Psalm 50:13 are examples) so the commandment could have been against "drinking blood" had God wished. What He commanded, however, was not to eat meat that had not been bled. One of the many verses where we see this is 1 Samuel 14:34:

> "…Bring me hither every man his ox, and every man

his sheep, and slay them here, and eat; and sin not against the LORD in eating with the blood..."

When an animal was slaughtered, the blood was to be drained out onto the ground.

"Only thou shalt not eat the blood thereof; thou shalt pour it upon the ground as water" (Deut. 15:23).

Blood Was Prohibited Primarily to the Jews

These commandments in the Old testament were primarily given to Jews living before Christ:

"Speak unto the children of Israel, saying... Moreover ye shall eat no manner of blood, whether it be of fowl or of beast, in any of your dwellings. Whatsoever soul it be that eateth any manner of blood, even that soul shall be cut off from his people" (Lev. 7:23-27).

Gentiles Who Lived with the Jews Were also Prohibited from Eating Blood

The commandment not to eat blood, however, applied not only to the Jews, but also to those Gentiles who lived among them in their land.

"Therefore I said unto the children of Israel, No soul of you shall eat blood, neither shall any stranger that sojourneth among you eat blood" (Lev. 17:12).

As the passage continues, it also excludes eating animals which had died of themselves. These animals had not been bled (17:15).

Other Gentiles Could Eat Blood

Gentiles who were not residents among the Jews were permitted to eat blood. In fact, it was stipulated in the law that the Jews could give or sell meat to them even if it had not been properly bled:

"Ye shall not eat of any thing that dieth of itself: thou shalt give it unto the stranger that is in thy gates, that he may eat it; or thou mayest sell it unto an alien: for thou art an holy people unto the LORD thy God..." (Deut. 14:21).

Which Are You?

Most Jehovah's witnesses today are neither Jews, nor residents in Jewish countries, but fit the category of those gentiles who were permitted to eat blood.

The Reason for the Law about Blood

There may well be health related reasons for not eating meat that has not been bled, but if there are, they are not stated. God gives us another reason:

"For the life of the flesh is in the blood: and I have given it to you upon the altar to make an atonement for your souls: for it is the blood that maketh an atonement for the soul" (Lev. 17:11).

The word translated "life" in the first part of this verse is the normal word for "soul" and is translated in different ways depending on the context. In "life of the flesh" it seems to be used in the sense of that which gives life to the flesh. God says that it is the blood which does this.

The phrase: "I have given it to you upon the altar to make an atonement for your souls," is probably significant. God had certainly commanded the priests to offer blood of the sacrificed animals upon the altar in the Old Testament sacrificial system. Here, however, He says, "I have given it," rather than that He has commanded someone else to give it. This probably infers that He is looking beyond the Old Testament to another sacrifice that He Himself was going to give. The Old Testament sacrifices were themselves a prophecy of the sacrifice of Christ. In saying "I have given it" Jehovah was probably looking forward to this final sacrifice which He Himself would make on the cross.

In Hebrews 10:1, in the middle of an explanation that Christ's one perfect sacrifice had replaced the Old Testament sacrifices, these sacrifices are called "a shadow of good things to come." The passage goes on to explain that Christ's sacrifice was sufficient to pay for all of our sins, and thus had no need to be repeated. It is the means God chose for our salvation and as such, was foreshadowed by the Old Testament sacrifices.

Please read all of Hebrews chapters nine and ten with great attention. You will find the reason for the commandment about blood. To save space, I will only give a small taste of this vital and fascinating passage that helps us understand and believe:

• "So Christ was once offered to bear the sins of many; and unto them that look for him shall he appear the second time without sin unto salvation. For the law having a shadow of good things to come, and not the very image of the things, can never with those sacrifices which they offered year by year continually make the comers thereunto perfect" (Heb. 9:28-10:1).

The old Testament sacrifices had to be repeated, but: "we are sanctified through the offering of the body of Jesus Christ once for all" (Heb. 10:10). His sacrifice did not need to be repeated.

• "And every priest standeth daily ministering and offering oftentimes the same sacrifices, which can never take away sins: But this man, after he had offered one sacrifice for sins for ever, sat down on the right hand of God" (Heb. 10:11-12).

The blood that God gave for sin on the Old Testament altar was a type, or foretelling of what He was going to pour out for us once and for all on the cross and as such was not to be taken lightly or dishonored. Be careful not to miss out on Jehovah's atonement for your sins, the reason he cared about blood.

May We Eat Blood Now?

In the New Testament, God put more emphasis on the Spirit of the law than on the letter, and permitted His people to eat many things that he had not let the Jews eat:

• "For every creature of God is good, and nothing to be refused, if it be received with thanksgiving for it is sanctified by the word of God and prayer" (1 Tim. 4:4-5).

• "I know, and am persuaded by the Lord Jesus, that there is nothing unclean of itself: but to him that esteemeth any thing to be unclean, to him it is unclean" (Rom. 14:14).

The Decision of the Apostles

Nevertheless, at the conference in Jerusalem when it was decided that the Gentile Christians should not be required to observe the Old Testament laws, a few exceptions to this liberty were made. One of these exceptions was that the Gentile Christians should abstain from blood.

> "But that we write unto them, that they abstain from pollutions of idols, and from fornication, and from things strangled, and from blood. For Moses of old time hath in every city them that preach him, being read in the synagogues every sabbath day" (Acts 15:20-21).

This passage seems to infer that Christians should not eat blood because it would offend the Jews who lived among them. Is this the only reason?

Before the Law

Probably not, because even before the birth of Abraham, the founder of the Hebrew race, when Jews did not yet exist, the commandment to bleed meat that is being slaughtered was given to Noah:

"But flesh with the life thereof, which is the blood thereof, shall ye not eat" (Gen. 9:4).

Probably even this passage looked forward to the precious blood of the Lord Jesus Christ which would pay for all men's sins, and it was given long before the law.

Transfusions

Eating meat that has not been bled is much different than giving or receiving blood transfusions. When our blood might help someone, should we give it or not give it? The Bible does not specifically address the problem of transfusions, but it does give glimpses into God's heart that show us what He wants us to do in these cases. Some of Christ's experiences will help us decide whether we should give blood or not:

"And he was teaching in one of the synagogues on the sabbath. And, behold, there was a woman which had a spirit of infirmity eighteen years, and was bowed together, and could in no wise lift up herself. And when Jesus saw her, he called her to him, and said unto her, Woman, thou art loosed from thine infirmity. And he laid his hands on her: and immediately she was made straight, and glorified God. And the ruler of the synagogue answered with indignation, because that Jesus had healed on the sabbath day, and said unto the people, There are six days in which men ought to work: in them therefore come and be healed, and not on the sabbath day. The Lord then answered him, and said, Thou hypocrite, doth not each one of you on the sabbath loose his ox or his ass from the stall, and lead him away to watering? And ought not this woman, being a daughter of Abraham, whom Satan hath bound, lo, these eighteen years, be loosed from this bond on the sabbath day" (Luke 13:10-16)?

This case is similar to that of giving blood because Jesus was doing something to help people which was interpreted by the religious leaders as being against the law of Moses. Did Jesus give in and say, "Oh, I hadn't thought of it that way. I won't do it again?" No! On the contrary, he called them hypocrites. He showed them that leading their ox from the stall on the Sabbath to give it a drink, which they had never thought God intended the law to prohibit, would have been just as much against the law as healing. Jesus was teaching that it is always important to do good things for people. God does not oppose doing good, and His law should not be interpreted as if He did.

Another important passage in understanding whether we should give or receive blood is Matthew 12:10-12:

"And, behold, there was a man which had his hand withered. And they asked him, saying, Is it lawful to heal on the sabbath days? that they might accuse him. And he said unto them, What man shall there be among you, that shall have one sheep, and if it fall into a pit on the sabbath day, will he not lay hold on it, and lift it out? How much then is a man better than a sheep? Wherefore it is lawful to do well on the sabbath days."

While neither of these illustrations deals directly with the problem of transfusions, they both point out that it is lawful to do good things; that God is interested in people and does not want us to use our interpretation of the law as a reason to avoid helping them.

On another occasion when Jesus was accused of doing something against the law He said:

> "...I will ask you one thing; Is it lawful on the sabbath days to do good, or to do evil? to save life, or to destroy it?" (Luke 6:9).

Jesus then healed a man, and the religious leaders, infuriated, started planning how to get rid of him. If you do the right thing, some might turn against you like they did against Jesus. Do it anyway!

Christ helped us understand a very important principle: the law was given to help people, to get people to do good and not evil. The law encourages us to save lives, but sometimes withholding blood actually amounts to killing. What would you do if your child were in an accident and lost so much blood that without a transfusion he would die and you had the right type blood to save him? Would you save the life, or kill? Those who twist the law and tell you, "You should not give blood, even when it will save a life!" do not understand the important underlying principles of the Bible, but have taken its words in the same superficial way that the Pharisees did. Like them, they end up contradicting what God teaches us to do.

Another time, Christ's disciples picked grain and ate it

on the sabbath. When the religious leaders complained to him, Jesus replied:

> "And he said unto them, The sabbath was made for man, and not man for the sabbath: Therefore the Son of man is Lord also of the sabbath" (Mark 2:27,28).

Love Fulfills the Whole Law

Though I have used the sabbath to illustrate, the Bible gives this type of explanation to the entire law:

> "Owe no man any thing, but to love one another: for he that loveth another hath fulfilled the law. For this, Thou shalt not commit adultery, Thou shalt not kill, Thou shalt not steal, Thou shalt not bear false witness, Thou shalt not covet; and if there be any other commandment, it is briefly comprehended in this saying, namely, Thou shalt love thy neighbour as thyself. Love worketh no ill to his neighbour: therefore love is the fulfilling of the law" (Rom. 13:8-10).

The Jews who accused Christ had not understood the basic purpose of the law.

Do you wonder what God wants you to do? Ask yourself, "Which course of action will show love?" That is the one which will fulfill the law. If I, by giving a bit of my blood, may help someone, I should do it.

> "Withhold not good from them to whom it is due, when it is in the power of thine hand to do it" (Prov. 3:27).

Religious leaders today who tell us the opposite have fallen into the same trap as the ones in Jesus' times. Not understanding the spirit of the law, they act contrary to the overall intent of the law, trying to fulfill what they think is the letter of the law. We should get this principle straight:

"For all the law is fulfilled in one word, even in this; Thou shalt love thy neighbour as thyself" (Gal. 5:14).

Be a Good Neighbor

Now that you have read the explanation, let's see what you will do. Here is a situation: Your neighbor's wife comes running over to your house and cries out, "My husband has been hit by a car! They found him lying beside the road bleeding to death. It's an emergency! He needs your type blood immediately!" This could happen to you tomorrow. If it does, what will you do?

Here is a story that Jesus told which will help you make up your mind:

"And Jesus answering said, A certain man went down from Jerusalem to Jericho, and fell among thieves, which stripped him of his raiment, and wounded him, and departed, leaving him half dead. And by chance there came down a certain priest that way: and when he saw him, he passed by on the other side. And likewise a Levite, when he was at the place, came and looked on him, and passed by on the other side. But a certain Samaritan, as he journeyed, came where he was: and when he saw him, he had compassion on him, and went to him, and bound up his wounds, pouring in oil and wine, and set him on his own beast, and brought him to an inn, and took care of him. And on the morrow when he departed, he took out two pence, and gave them to the host, and said unto him, Take care of him; and whatsoever thou spendest more, when I come again, I will repay thee. Which now of these three, thinkest thou, was neighbour unto him that fell among the thieves? And he said, He that shewed mercy on him. Then said Jesus unto him, Go, and do thou likewise" (Luke 10:30-37).

While your neighbor may not have come running over yet, you are still faced with the decision. Will you follow the religious leaders and pass by on the other side, or will you be a good neighbor who shows love to those who need help?

Partly because Jesus explained the law this way, the religious leaders of his day decided to get rid of Him by having Him killed (Mark 3:4-6).

Killing Christ did not work well at all, so some in our day try to get rid of Him by saying, "He was not God!" "He was not really resurrected!" "He does not really save!"

If you do this too, repent right now, trust the Savior to save you and to give you the ability to live for Him!

And this is the record, that God hath given to us eternal life, and this life is in his Son. He that hath the Son hath life; and he that hath not the Son of God hath not life. 1 John 5:11-12

12

Your Key to the Kingdom

How can you get into Paradise where God reigns? Will your answer be a repeat of what so many man made religions teach? I asked you a similar question at the beginning of the first chapter. Has your reading made a difference, or are you still counting largely on the things you do? Are you trying to accomplish certain tasks or counting on being able to live by a set of rules that you will never succeed in following?

God gave rules in the Old Testament law that showed men how they should live but men did not live that way. Then when people sinned God had them sacrifice animals as a foreshadowing or preview of what Christ was going to do. Later He sent Jesus as the final sacrifice. He paid the entire penalty for all of our sins. The New Testament tells us that God's laws do not show us how good we are, but what we have done wrong. They show us our sinfulness, but don't give the power to live as God wishes. They turn us to Christ who saves by showing us that we can't save ourselves.

Good Works Don't Save. The Savior Saves!

God says:

"Therefore by the deeds of the law there shall no flesh be justified in his sight: for by the law is the knowledge of sin. But now the righteousness of God without the law is manifested, being witnessed by the law and the prophets; even the righteousness of God which is by faith of Jesus Christ unto all and upon all them that believe: for there is no difference: For all have sinned, and come short of the glory of God" (Rom. 3:20-23).

A young Jehovah's Witness asked me, "Does this mean that all those things which I have done are worth nothing toward my salvation?" Rather than respond myself, I quoted another New Testament Epistle:

"I do not frustrate the grace of God: for if righteousness come by the law, then Christ is dead in vain" (Gal. 2:21).

Do you shove aside the grace of God who is offering you salvation in Christ to try to save yourself by God's law or by the rules of the Watchtower? If so, how can you ever be sure you have done enough?

Perhaps you realize that not all your works have been good ones, and are counting on a mix of your works and God's grace. Jehovah says:

"And if by grace, then is it no more of works: otherwise grace is no more grace. But if it be of works, then is it no more grace: otherwise work is no more work" (Rom. 11:6).

If salvation is given to us who don't deserve it by God's grace, it is not earned by our works. If you are trusting that your works count for at least part of your salvation, you are not trusting Christ to save you. You are like the drowning person that thrashes around so much that he won't let the person who has come to save him do it.

God wants to save you by His grace, through His Son. There is no other salvation. This matter is so important that I beg you to carefully study also: Acts 4:12; 13:37-39; Rom. 3:20-28; 4:16; 5:20-21; Gal. 3:1-19; 2 Tim. 1:9; Titus 3:5-7.

A Second Chance?

Some hope that after the resurrection there will be a second chance. They refer to Revelation 20 which tells of the judgment before the great white throne. Here people are judged for their works. Don't just take one of these verses out of context. The chapter builds up to the climax:

"...and they were judged every man according to their works. And death and hell were cast into the lake of fire. This is the second death. And **whosoever was not found written in the book of life was cast into the lake of fire**" (Rev. 20:15).

Not one was found with works good enough to merit life. Only those whose names were in the book of life were saved. This is judgment. There is no second chance. Your name is written in the Lamb's Book of Life at the time that you accept Christ in this life, or it is not there.

The Reason We Cannot Earn Any of Our Salvation Is Because It Is a Gift of God

• "For by grace are ye saved through faith; and that not of yourselves: **it is the gift of God, not of works,** lest any man should boast" (Eph. 2:8-9).

• "And this is the record, that God hath given to us eternal life, and this life is in his Son. He that hath the Son hath life; and he that hath not the Son of God hath not life" (1 John 5:11-12). A gift cannot be earned. One must decide to receive it. You may decide right now to receive God's gift.

We Receive God's Gift of Salvation through Faith in Jesus Christ

"But as many as received him, to them gave he power to become the sons of God, even to them that believe on his name, which were born, not of blood, nor of the will of the flesh, nor of the will of man, but of God" (John 1:12-13).

To enter God's reign, we must be born of Him by trusting Christ the Savior to save us!

A Purified Life Is the Result, Not the Cause of Salvation

• God said that our salvation is not a reward for our works, but a gift that He gives us when we trust Christ to save us. Immediately afterward He added:

"For we are his workmanship, created in Christ Jesus unto good works, which God hath before ordained that we should walk in them" (Eph. 2:10).

God works in those who have been saved by grace that they might do good works.

• "Who gave himself for us, that he might redeem us from all iniquity, and purify unto himself a peculiar people, zealous of good works" (Titus 2:14).

• "Therefore if any man be in Christ, he is a new creature: old things are passed away; behold, all things are become new" (2 Cor. 5:17).

Act!

It is spiritual suicide to keep following doctrines that can't save and go against some of the most vital points of God's Word. We have seen from their books that the people who established Jehovah's Witness' doctrine made many mistakes interpreting the Bible. You must choose whether you will trust the system set up by these men who can't save, and don't interpret the Bible accurately, or put your faith in the real Christ of the Bible to save you:

"Who was delivered for our offenses, and was raised again for our justification" (Rom. 4:25).

If you receive the Savior and the salvation that only He can give, He will forgive your sins and make you a child in His family, giving you eternal life. In addition, you will receive the power of the Holy Spirit which will enable you to live a life which pleases God.

To choose to follow Watchtower doctrines in the crucial area of how to become one of God's people, is to reject Jehovah's provision for your salvation.

> "Jesus answered and said unto him, Verily, verily, I say unto thee, Except a man be born again, he cannot see the kingdom of God" (John 3:3).

It is that simple! People say you can get in without being born again but God says you can't. Who is it that reigns? God, or do they? Then who has the right to decide how you can enter?

Shift your faith! Stop believing your actions can save you and put your trust in the Savior to do it.

When you have decided, you may want to thank God for His gift of salvation with a prayer like this: "Father, I have sinned, and I believe that Christ came to save sinners. Right now I trust Jesus Christ to save me. I thank you that He has taken all my sins onto Himself and clothed me in His righteousness."

At this point it would be good to confess to God all the sins you can remember having done. Trust Christ to save you from each one of them and from the ones you can't remember too. Then thank God that the blood of the Lord Jesus Christ has washed away all your sins.

If you still haven't decided to trust Christ alone to

save you, please go back and read the first chapter again. Then come back and read this chapter prayerfully, again and again, until you, too, understand, and are born spiritually through faith in Christ.

"And that every tongue should confess that Jesus Christ is Lord, to the glory of God the Father" (Phlp. 2:11).

ALSO BY THOMAS HEINZE

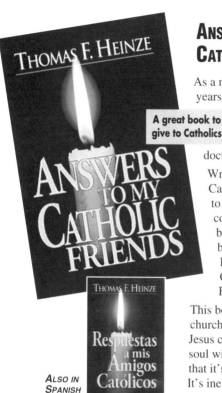

A great book to give to Catholics

ALSO IN SPANISH

ANSWERS THAT CAN LEAD CATHOLICS TO CHRIST

As a missionary in Italy for over thirty years, Thomas Heinze found that the ecumenical movement has caused Catholics to have questions about Protestant doctrine and the Bible.

Written lovingly to the Roman Catholics, this book uses Scriptures to provide clear, honest answers concerning major differences between Catholic and Protestant beliefs. To increase effectiveness, Heinze quotes from the Catholic's own New American Bible.

This book shows Catholics that their church cannot save… only faith in Jesus can. It contains such a loving, soul winning message and invitation that it's a great book to give Catholics. It's inexpensive too!

62 pages, paperback

ANSWERS QUESTIONS THAT CATHOLICS OFTEN ASK:

- Where do the differences between Catholics and Protestants come from?
- What is the most important difference between Protestants and Catholics?
- Why don't Protestants venerate images?
- Why are Evangelical pastors permitted to marry?
- Do you have a Mass like us?

- Do you believe in Mary?
- Is there a purgatory?
- On whom is the Church founded?
- To whom should we confess our sins?